How to move minds and influence people

How to move minds and influence people

A remarkable way of engaging and persuading others

Iain Carruthers

London • New York • Toronto • Sydney • Tokyo • Singapore
Hong Kong • Cape Town • Madrid • Paris • Amsterdam • Munich • Milan

PEARSON EDUCATION LIMITED

Head Office
Edinburgh Gate
Harlow CM20 2JE
Tel: +44 (0)1279 623623
Fax: +44 (0)1279 431059

London Office:
128 Long Acre
London WC2E 9AN
Tel: +44 (0)20 7447 2000
Fax: +44 (0)20 7447 2170
www.business-minds.com
www.yourmomentum.com

First published in Great Britain in 2003

ISBN 0 273 66336 4

British Library Cataloguing in Publication Data
A CIP catalogue record for this book can be obtained from the British Library

10 9 8 7 6 5 4 3 2 1

Designed by Sue Lamble
Typeset by Northern Phototypesetting Co. Ltd, Bolton
Printed and bound in Great Britain by Bell & Bain Ltd, Glasgow

The Publishers' policy is to use paper manufactured from sustainable forests.

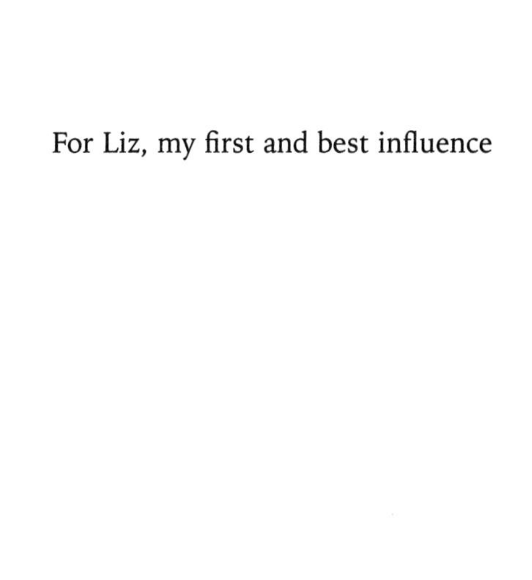

For Liz, my first and best influence

Contents

Acknowledgements

Like many people, I've daydreamed about writing a book. The fact that this has actually appeared is largely due to the help of three people. My wife Liz bundled the kids away every Saturday for the summer, and provided unending support. Rachael Stock at Pearson has, far too often, been praised by authors knocked out by her enthusiasm and passion for her trade. So I won't embarrass her again. And among a great faculty of teachers at Ashridge, I want to thank Robin Ladkin for his elegant but insistent promptings that I had something worth saying.

Books rely on great professionals to make them happen. Lesley Felce, Hannah Cottrill, Rachel Kay and the design skills of Sue Lamble made sure this one did. Andrzej Krauze's line illustrations often grace the pages of the *Guardian* and I'm lucky that they do so here.

The germ of this book was a conversation with Allan Marriott. Guy Browning helped me by opening his contacts book. Many others have helped, wittingly or unwittingly, by providing examples, ideas or simply arguing me out of wrong headed assumptions. They include Malcolm Evans, Mark Melluish, John Simmons, Colette Dorward, Hugh Pidgeon, Judy Young, John Thompson, Duncan Sedgwick, Mike Solloway, Tom Cunningham, Catriona Crombie, David Carroll, Claire Seabrook, Gordon Brown and Chris Hulse. Finally, for teaching me to write in the first place, along with so much else, my thanks to my mum and dad.

Preface

Gordon Brown and the White Fish Authority

I used to work for a market research company called Millward Brown. At staff meetings and conferences, one of the founders, Gordon Brown, would tell us a particular story. (No, not *that* Gordon Brown.)

Starting out in the sixties, he had been employed by a well-known research business which was doing rather badly. They shared a floor of an indifferent London office block with a government body – the White Fish Authority, which had about forty employees.

Every so often Gordon's firm had to lay off employees and abandon some office space. Every time, the partition moved along, and the White Fish people invaded the vacated space. It had never been clear what the White Fish Authority did, but it was clear there was increasing demand for it. Perhaps more people were needed to maintain authority over white fish. Whatever, that partition kept on moving.

That story served Millward Brown better than a hundred slides on the virtues of company growth. If he felt the audience needed it, Gordon would make the point that there are two sorts of business – ones that grow and ones that don't. And that no one wants to be invaded by a White Fish Authority.

Like any good entrepreneur, Gordon used stories. But he also had his own story. He wanted to make a difference – to bring a greater intelligence to business decisions. That was his drive (alongside the yacht he's probably sailing right now.)

Every one of us is able to make a difference. This book is about helping you create it by influencing others. We won't be doing it with fancy techniques or models. We'll be doing it by telling stories.

The book is structured in two acts: the first (Chapters 1–5) provides a set of ideas and tools to help you influence people in your working life. It demonstrates how you can use the craft of stories to tell your own business story and take others with you.

Act 2 (Chapters 6–9) looks at your own story. We'll put together where you've been, what you do and where you're headed.

Appendix 1 provides a trove of useful stories you can dip into to help you influence in the workplace. Appendix 2 looks further afield at other areas of your life where you can influence for good, focusing in particular on children and community action.

I'd be delighted to hear from any readers with feedback about the book and how you've used it. Or if you just fancy telling me a story.

Iain Carruthers
moveminds@encounterbusiness.com
January 2003

act 1

Stories at work

1

What's the story?

The hunger

It's chaos out there. And the worse it gets, the more we hunger for values and beliefs that endure. Stories are about what endures, despite change. That is why they have such importance and power. It's why they are so useful in influencing people, but more of that later on.

Hang on, you say, I thought stories were about change – about drama and conflict? Yes, indeed, but their purpose is to remind you about what keeps going. Without those anchors, we feel adrift. We cannot connect what is happening with the past and the future.

A story is there to meet a human need: to affirm an enduring quality or value. How we tell a story also meets a human need: to listen and connect.

In this book, we're going to reference some stories you may know. At different points in the book, we're going to dip into

> *“a story is there to meet a human need: to affirm an enduring quality or value”*

three films – *Erin Brockovich, American Beauty* and *The Shawshank Redemption*. It doesn’t matter if you’ve only seen one or two of them. (If you’ve managed to miss them all, I’ve got to question your credentials as a member of the human race.)

All sorts of extraordinary things happen in these films. But certain things endure.

What changes	What endures
Erin Brockovich A struggling single mother finds a job in a legal firm and becomes involved in a huge litigation against a power corporation, risking love and family in the process	Erin’s cussed belief in fairness
American Beauty A family man is fired from his job, falls for his daughter’s teenage friend, discovers his wife’s affair and is shot dead by the sexually thwarted father of his drug-dealing next door neighbour	Lester Burnham’s belief that life is to be relished
The Shawshank Redemption A professional man is wrongly imprisoned for the murder of his adulterous wife, spends 20 years in jail, where he is beaten up and raped, eventually escaping by extraordinary means	Andy DuFresne’s belief in survival on his own terms

Each film has, in the words of the screenwriter, a protagonist. It means, literally ‘first actor’ – the character who carries the meaning of the film.

PIT*STOP* Psychotherapy

There's an eminent psychotherapist, who, in his therapy, acts on the assumption that there is a novel in everyone's life. Can you imagine sitting down with someone who was dedicated to helping to understand the riveting drama of your life?

One of the tasks of psychotherapy is to help someone be aware of what is causing them to act in particular ways, especially ways that cause them anxiety or pain. The assumption is that there is some pattern of belief that has encouraged the actions the client has taken. Often, this pattern of belief is hidden from the person. What's driving the drama?

We watched these films in our millions. Why? They evoked wonder in us. We rooted for these people, because they enacted beliefs that we share, even (and especially) in the face of antagonistic forces. Inside, we wonder if we'd be brave enough to make the choices they did.

We need values, anchors for our lives. But it's difficult to identify with abstract qualities like justice, wonder and survival. We need them to be enacted by other human beings. We need stories to make them real. That's why, in this disconnected world of the twenty-first century, the hunger for story is so strong. We need beliefs that endure like we've never needed them before.

Getting unstuck

At this point, you're probably thinking 'Fine, but how does this help me to

1. run a project
2. lead a team

3 win a contract

4 get home on time . . . ?'

Let me explain. Each of these activities requires you to influence others, in order that you do them well. In fact, the success of any venture or activity you engage in is directly related to your ability to influence.

Influence is an awkward word for some. It can imply the manipulation of people for personal gain. And in the wrong hands, it can. Goebbels used stories, and pretty effectively too.

But let's look at the meaning of the word. *In-fluence* literally means being 'in flow', from the Latin *fluere*. What we're actually doing when we influence is helping people become unstuck. That strikes me as being pretty useful in all walks of life.

It's especially useful if you're trying to make something happen in an organization. If your job title includes the word manager, supervisor, executive, leader or director, your basic job is to help other people get things done. In order to do that, you need to influence them. (And even if you don't have such an august title, it's a fair bet that if you can't influence that well, you can't do your job that well either.)

There are many ways of influencing people. You can coax, flatter or even threaten them. However, the most potent way is by helping them to imagine how things could be different.

The story has been the tool of choice for influencers from day one. From caveman stories about animal magic, through the great myths of East and West, right down to the factory owner, teacher or supervisor persuading a recalcitrant group of people to take life into their own hands: each works to create a memorable picture of what is possible, if we did but choose to try.

Every successful story is a narrative of possibility. Its strength lies in the fact that it expresses belief in a value that endures, as

> *“the story has been the tool of choice for influencers from day one”*

acted out by a human *who could be you.* And that's almost irresistible. So if you are running a project, leading a team or trying to win a contract, think about this. What if you could get behind their scepticism or defences? What if they could see the world from your vantage, and enjoy the view? What if they could see just what was possible?

A story will help you.

2

Stories: express routes to influence

Where we learn how to connect with someone, discover the Law of Three, and get inside your boss's head

The short cut

Like a bolt out from the blue
Did you hear it too?

Prefab Sprout, I Remember That

As humans, we are magnets for experience. Our brain is an extraordinary recorder of these experiences. Almost everything gets logged. Imagine a library the size of a cathedral, stuffed with images, words, soundtracks, smells, people, landscapes, emotions. That's your mind. That's your friend's mind, your customer's mind, your boss's mind.

The brain has to develop ways of accessing what's in there quickly and reliably. If it didn't, we'd all be basket cases by next week. So we create short cuts – ways of accessing parts of our mind quickly and reliably. A little like the search function on a web site, although not always as reliable.

A few short cuts:

- Someone wearing your ex-partner's scent
- A picture of your mother or father as a child
- A particular song or poem
- A memory that comes to you from nowhere as you lie on the grass in a summer's day
- The words 'Once Upon a Time'

These are express routes to a feeling or memory. It could be a delightful memory or it could spear you in the gut.

Create an express route

“stories, used correctly, are express routes to connecting with someone”

The point is that stories, used correctly, are express routes to connecting with someone. They are a short cut to a more intimate part of the mind. They have been, in the past, and in our childhood, a fundamental way in which we understand the world. They smuggle their way straight into our brains.

The most influential people of history have often been outstanding storytellers. Christ’s parables were a short cut to the minds of his listeners. Taoism and Zen make constant use of stories. Islam has as its narrative the life and lessons of the Prophet Mohammed. In more recent times, outstanding political leaders such as Roosevelt and Churchill mastered the medium of radio to pull populations together.

Their ability was not to harangue people. It was to engage in a conversation that they guided.

Come with me

When we begin to tell a story, we take people to a different place. The words ‘Can I tell you a story?’ or ‘I’ve got a great story for you’ are almost impossible for a human being to resist.

Why? Well, you are offering a pass into an imagined world. A threshold. Just like when Alice in Wonderland found the vial saying ‘Drink Me’, you’re offering a sign saying ‘Come With Me’.

The important thing is not that this is an invitation to your imagination, but that it’s an invitation to your listener’s own mind. Their defences are down. They want to come on the journey.

PIT*STOP* The formula for the express route

This is one of those absolutely universal laws that we spend time trying to avoid, such as The Inland Revenue Will Make You Give Them Your Tax Return Eventually, or Your Mother Will Give You Advice on Rearing Your Children. But this is more important.

Connection = the stimulus you provide + the response provided by the listener

You cannot connect with someone by telling them the response you want from them.

Let me explain.

Option 1

If I want you to think I'm funny, I tell you a joke, or a few stories. You laugh. Inwardly, you think, 'he's quite funny'. Job done.

Option 2

If I want you to think I'm funny, I say to you 'I'm quite funny, me.' Inwardly, you think, 'you're a twat.'

Option 2 is the route almost universally taken by business leaders and their functionaries. It's at its peak in communication about business values. What is this obsession with telling other people that we've got values? No, we really have. Come on, you've been there. *Our values are integrity, customer focus and teamwork.* Sure we've just cut six corners on our supply chain, junked the customer service targets and fired half the Runcorn plant, but these truly are our values. If the business/public service world stopped proclaiming their values (telling us the response they want) and devoted a little time to doing stuff that proves it (the stimulus that allows us to respond), this little world would be a better place. Or at least less cynical.

If you're in an interview, and you want someone to believe that you're devoted to customer service, for heaven's sake don't *tell* them you're devoted to customer service. Treat them to an ▶

engaging example of something you've done (stimulus) that let's them draw the conclusion (response) that you're nuts about delivering to people.

When in the US, I interviewed someone who wanted to switch careers from sales to marketing. He'd worked at Nordstrom, the department store in the States notorious for its devotion to a good service experience. (There's a story about a Nordstrom store taking back a set of tyres from a customer, even though they, Nordstrom, don't sell tyres. Who knows? It ought to be true.) This guy, prompted by the fact that he was speaking to a Brit, told me what had happened the other weekend.

I had this English guy come onto the menswear floor, asking for a clip-on bowtie – he had some function he had to go to. Now we hadn't stocked up those and only had regular tie-up bow ties. So I could have let it go, but we're always encouraged to invest time with a customer, so I said, 'Look if you can spare 10 minutes, I'll teach you how to tie a bow tie. We'll have solved your problem for tonight, and you'll always know how to do it.' He grinned and said okay, so we stood there and practised it for 15 minutes till he could do it. He was delighted, picked up three shirts and another tie and I had the commission off $300, not $20 for a bow tie.

Compare that with someone staring at you saying 'I always try and go out of my way for customers' and you see the difference between stimulus and response.

Can I tell you a story?

This was told by a gentleman called Milton Erickson. He used it to introduce his belief that as adults, many of us intuitively know our way in life or in a job, and we need to trust that instinct a little more. Take a moment to read it through.

The Horse on the Road

When I was a young man, we lived in the country. One day a horse wandered into our family's yard. The horse had no identifying marks, and no one knew whom it belonged to. I didn't have much to do that day so I said I'd try and find out whose it was.

I got on the horse and rode it back to the road. I got this notion that I would let the horse decide which way it wanted to go. From time to time the horse wandered off the road or stopped to graze in a field. When that happened, I'd gently direct it back onto the road.

Eventually, the horse stopped outside a farmhouse, several miles down the road. The farmer came out, thanked me for returning him and asked 'How did you know that was our horse and that he belonged here?'

'I didn't', I said, 'but the horse did. All I did was keep him on the road.'

Let's look at what's happening here.

Where did you go? The chances are that you crossed the threshold with Erickson. You then travelled in his company. You saw a young man in blue jeans puzzling over this mystery horse, and following his instincts about what it might do. You might have seen or heard him geeing the horse on from its frequent stops for grazing. Those of you who have ridden might have felt the muscle memory of riding, with its alternating freedom and tension. You might have seen him dismounting, perhaps patting the horse and wandering home back along the road.

You may have experienced less than this, or a whole lot more.

You've just participated in a story. We seem to need this journeying. We gladly exchange the here and now for the journey, especially if is crafted well for us. Why else do we queue up *“stories are there to guide, not preach”*

in our millions for the experience of films, soap operas and fiction?

You might have noticed something else. The teller of this story had a proposition – that humans are the best judges of where they need to be and what they want to do. But a proposition without a narrative is a sorry thing. If someone has a proposition for you, your natural instinct is to think ‘what’s he trying to sell me?’ Your defences go up and your affence flick on. A narrative or story seduces you into listening, and gets the proposition working away at a deeper, more satisfying level.

We hunger for stories. They can take us to worlds beyond ourselves. And with great writing, music, movies or television, we don’t just go to the world, we play in it, we identify with it, we imagine ourselves there.

Think of one of the films I mentioned earlier. The writer of *Erin Brockovich* has a proposition: the ‘little people’ – those without ready access to power, money or the law – are often exploited and should have their rights upheld. Excuse me if I nod off, because that’s beginning to sound like a *Guardian* reader. However, embody the conflict in a woman’s struggle for her own soul and dignity while she fights for others, get the dialogue crackling, hire in Julia Roberts, then you’re beyond a proposition. You’re in a story.

Only connect

Forget the idea that the story is an easy way to get someone to think what you want them to think. It’s a way of having a deeper and better conversation than you might otherwise have. You

PITSTOP Theory: talking at or talking with?

This book is light on theory and deliberately so, but bear with me for three minutes.

One theory: talking at

There is a view of the world, sustained by the advertising business, that communicating with someone is about putting ideas into their heads. Target them, message them, educate them. It's based on the idea that influence works like this:

I have wisdom.
You have empty head.
I put wisdom in your empty head.
You act on my wisdom and go to supermarket.

I exaggerate for effect, but this is actually the assumption behind most people's idea of communicating. Just sit down and listen, you at the back.

Imagine a series of roundabouts, all with traffic backed up, all stalling. That's the state of communication in many of our businesses today. Not so much I Am Right, You Are Wrong, but I Think I May Be Right And Will You Just Let Me Through Here Because I Have Another Meeting At Three. That's talking at.

Another theory: talking with

Talking with someone is an entirely different ball of wax. Talking with them allows you to exercise influence, but in a more respectful and more effective fashion. It invites someone to respond to what you are saying, not just be there when you're saying it.

Since we were little, communicating has been about responding to one another. I say to Kate, my 18-month-old daughter 'Daddy'. She says 'Dada'. And we go on for a while. That's how she learns. A response calls forth another response, and a theme develops. It's how we all learn, until we join organizations. Then we sit down and watch people give presentations.

can't put new stuff in people's heads; they're already stuffed to the brim. You can only work with what's already there. Stories are there to guide, not preach.

The Law of Three

There are only three questions you need to ask yourself to start connecting:

1. What do you know about the people you want to influence?
2. What, specifically, do you want them to think or do?
3. What story would help them step up to this?

1 What do you know about the people you want to influence?

This is the first rule of the storyteller. You need to understand and empathize with the people you want to influence. You don't have to agree with them, or even like them much. But you do need an intuitive sense of their goals, needs and fears. Otherwise how can you hope to connect?

A friend of mine consulted to an Italian manufacturing company making motor bikes and scooters. Managers were concerned about the number of defects and recalls in the production process, and the safety implications for the bikes on the road. Quality workshops were held, ideas were encouraged, board directors came to speak. Newsletters went out. But little happened – defects were still at an unmanageable rate.

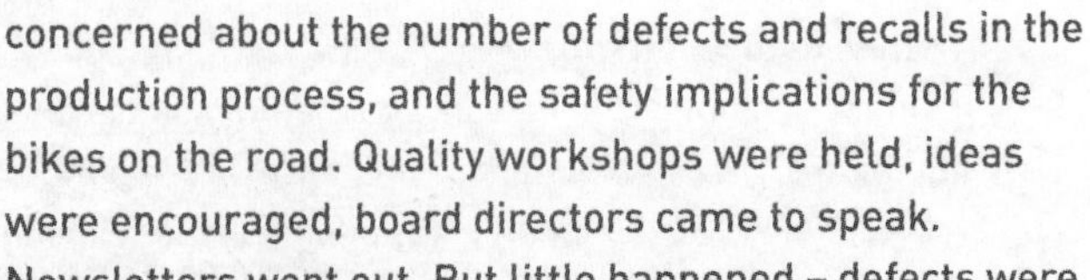

Then one of the managers had an idea over a family dinner. What was most important to him, he realized, was the protection and nurture of his family, especially his teenage children on the verge of adulthood – the very market for the bikes they produced. That was what he had in common with the workers in the factory. In the following week, he cancelled all the 'Quality' activity and communication. The week after that, he went around after the evening shift, placing a series of posters at visible points. The posters read simply, 'Someone's child will ride the bike you are making today'.

The mood changed. Production slowed as people began to double check their work, or challenge others' practices. When the workshops were re-introduced, there was an energy for quality unimaginable in the past. All because one man had taken the trouble to connect.

Try this simple exercise.

Take a moment, one minute maximum, to imagine the person/ people you want to connect to. Take a look at the world from their angle. Imagine yourself as them arriving at work – what's buzzing around in your mind? What do you suspect (or know) that their needs or fears might be? If you don't know, who might be able to tell you?

If you have the chance, and it's appropriate, ask them what they are seeking. What are their expectations from your encounter? What part of their larger story is this encounter?

Doodle these down. I find it easier to doodle using a simple mind map, where you put the person at the centre.

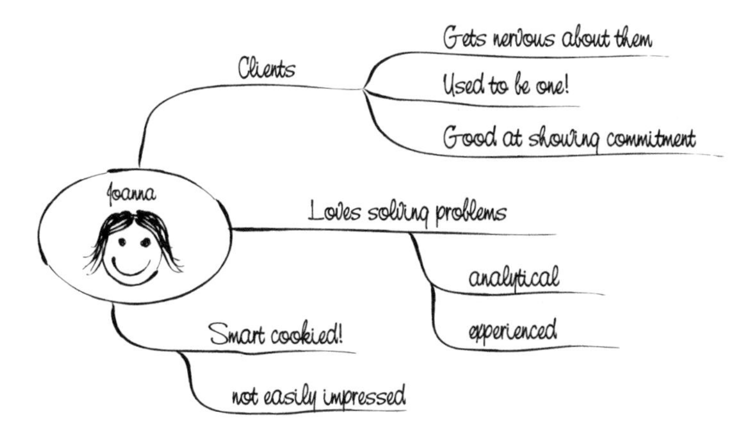

This will tell you much of what you need to know. Be sure you have a sense of:

1. The person's general view of the world – and if it's to do with work, their view of their role or responsibility.
2. That person's psychological needs, as far as you can guess. Do they enjoy humour, playfulness? Do they value tenacity or duty? Are they buttoned up or chilled out? Big picture/ little picture? Do they like to chat things out or internally process stuff?
3. What they are trying to achieve (if they know) and how this encounter may be part of that story.

Take the trouble to connect

And one other thing. Trust your judgement and your gut about this person. Then take the trouble to connect.

Alan Ball who wrote *American Beauty* had, I suspect, a very clear sense of the person he was writing for. Someone who felt trapped, even if the prison was comfortable. Someone who had lost their relish for life. Someone who would respond to the story of a man who, just in time, remembers what it's like to live.

2 What, specifically, do you want them to think or do?

You have a proposition to put to someone. Be clear and conservative about it. If you're trying to address an important or delicate issue, it's unlikely you're going to overturn 30 years of ingrown prejudice in half an hour. Even if you're speaking with people you know and trust, you're probably trying to take them somewhere they wouldn't normally go.

I'm sorry, but I'm going to use a bit of jargon here. When commercial writers create ideas and stories (for radio, TV or press) they try to *provoke reappraisal*. They know they're not going to change people's minds in one 30-second slot (despite my nasty aside about the advertising industry above). What they're trying to do is to seduce, nudge or jolt you into looking at a topic differently, provoking you into a reappraisal of that company or product.

Let's say you are a writer creating a magazine ad for a homeless charity. A realistic objective is to stimulate the reader into thinking 'That's worth thinking about', not 'God, I must transfer my life savings now, where's the bank?'

The same thinking applies to you. Imagine you want to negotiate a rise, or increased reward for someone in your team (Paul). You know your boss isn't going to roll over and cough up straightaway, so you have to set up a particular goal for the conversation. So be clear and conservative. Make your goal that they'll agree to a proposal from you.

John Lennon, in the early days, was the leader and setter of priorities for the Beatles. He later recalled that in their early days (1960-62) they never thought about being the best band in the world. 'We used to have this thing where I'd shout "Where are we going lads?" and they'd shout "To the toppermost of the poppermost", but mostly we just worked on being the best band that night. That was enough to cope with. After that we wanted to be the best in the Cavern and after that the best in Liverpool.'

3 What story would help them step up to this?

Let's assume that some form of story or parallel is going to help you make your case (in the vast majority of cases, it will). The selection and telling of this story is the cornerstone of this book.

There are three types of stories open to you. (Well, there are dozens, but life's too short. These will do for 90 per cent of any sane person's needs.) Let's look in turn at each of these three categories: parables, catalysts and tales.

Parables	*Definition*: A story with a mythic or universal quality, with its lesson embodied in the telling, but open to some interpretation. *Example*: Gordon Brown and The White Fish Authority/ The Horse on The Road (see pp. ix and 13). Parables can be potent. They are the modern versions of the tales and fables that helped us build civilizations. However, they have to be used wisely, otherwise you can end up sounding a bit of an arse. They are better used in formal or semi-formal situations, when you are addressing an audience or workshop. They can also be used in smaller groups, when you sense that you have authority to experiment.

Catalysts

Definition: A simple bare story, with little texture, but gains its resonance by the teller drawing out the implications for the audience.

Example: Mostly specific to your organization.

This type of story has been described well by Steve Denning in his book *The Springboard*. Essentially, it's a story that smuggles within it the type of change you are advocating to a business, the implications of which you then draw out. Denning believes that simplicity and bareness are essential, especially when others may be wary of your message.

Tales

Definition: More richly characterized stories, often comic, which embody and celebrate characteristics of a person or organization.

Example: John Varley Loses His Trousers (see Appendix 1).

Tales are what normally circulate in an organization and closer to what you naturally tell your colleagues. They have the ability to capture a moment or ethic. They tend to have different charges – positive (idealist), negative or comic/ironic.

They are particularly useful in informal situations, where you are seeking to gain rapid contact with someone and get them attuned to a world or idea. For example, the John Varley story was often told in Barclays as a way of showing how apparently remote figures are human, vulnerable and capable of being related to.

Now, all these stories have certain things in common. They have a protagonist: a person facing a predicament and choosing to act. The protagonist will often be involved in a conflict between her energy and her fear, choosing to use the former and confront the latter. The predicament is resolved in a way that embodies the kind of change you are seeking. By telling the story, you are inviting someone into that world so that they can respond to it from within themselves.

Let's take again the example of the team member for whom you're lobbying. I've based this loosely on a real-life example at a former company.

1	What do you know about the people you want to influence?	I'm going to assume you know your boss reasonably well. But have you looked at this from her point of view? What's in it for her to reward this member of the team – morale, retention of a team member, not being hassled by you? What parts of her personality or psychology can you appeal to? Let's assume you've done your homework and understood commitment to clients/customers is something that really drives her and is what she admires in others. Interestingly, it's also where a lot of the tension between her energy and fear is located.
2	What, specifically, do you want them to think or do?	Like we said earlier, she's not going to fold and authorize a 20 per cent raise before lunch. She, and the system, need longer. So perhaps your first goal is to get her to the point where she'll accept a proposal from you that argues a case.
3	What story would help them step up to this?	You've established two things. Your boss admires client commitment. She also needs to be in a frame of mind whereby she'll accept a proposal from you. You need a story

to soften her up and provoke reappraisal of Paul's needs. Ideally, this would be about how this team member shows the right stuff. All you need to do is to be able to describe it in a compelling way.

Fortunately . . .

Paul's story

I believe that one of the main reasons this team is delivering is Paul's contribution, but since he's not the type to shout about it, it tends not to get noticed. But can I tell you something about Paul?

You know how difficult it can be to work with X client? Well, the main guy's support team was really struggling with some of our recommendations. Paul was getting grief because they're the people he deals with on a regular basis. Two weeks ago, I found out that Paul had sweated over Sunday to get his head round the figures, and took it upon himself to go and work with the support team face to face for a few hours. He didn't make a fuss about it, but they did. They thought it was fantastic.

It's a simple story, but it has all the ingredients you need. Someone finds themselves in a predicament, used their skill and will to discover a resolution good for all parties. You've also told a story that embodies what is important to your audience (a client-committed boss) and how that person is delivering. As you tell it, you are inviting her on a journey to a place she has been – under pressure, with demanding clients and pressing deadlines – and having her identify with Paul. You've smuggled him in.

And once she has identified, or empathized with Paul, it's that much more difficult to put up the shutters to rewarding him. It would be like putting up the shutters to herself.

> *“sow a little FUD – Fear Uncertainty and Doubt – it always helps”*

It's your job to press home the advantage you've gained and ask her to consider a proposal on how he could be encouraged to continue and show more of this, especially as you suspect he's being head-hunted by another company. (Sow a little FUD – Fear Uncertainty and Doubt – it always helps.)

In the table below, you can see how the story is structured.

I believe that one of the main reasons this team is delivering is Paul's contribution, but since he's not the type to shout about it, it tends not to get noticed. But can I tell you something about Paul?	**Beginning: set up** Preps the audience for the story's relevance. Introduces the protagonist, with an invitation that can't be refused
You know how difficult it can be to work with X client?	References audience's own experience
Well, the main client's support team was really struggling with some of our recommendations. Paul was getting grief because they're the people he deals with on a regular basis.	**Middle** The **predicament or crisis** facing our hero – which is imaginable for the audience
Two weeks ago, I found out that Paul had sweated over Sunday to get his head round the figures, and took it upon himself to go and work with the support team face to face for a few hours.	**End** The **predicament is resolved by** a choice and course of action and struggle. The action reflects his active value
He didn't make a fuss about it, but they did. They thought it was fantastic.	**The result** of the activity – reflecting audience's concern about client satisfaction. Drawing out of implications.

Summary

In this chapter, we've taken up the basic tools of storytelling and started to get to grips with them.

We've looked at how you go about preparing yourself to connect: understand the audience, know what it is you want them to do or think, and finding a story that will help them step up to it.

We've also looked at how you can structure a story: the beginning (set up), middle (predicament or crisis) and end (resolution or result) – and then, should you need to, draw out the implications.

3

More expressways

Where we explore the time and place to use story to influence

Presentations

Let's start off by banning that word, shall we? It won't be easy, since it infects business and organizational life. 'Have you finished that presentation?' 'They're coming up for the presentation tomorrow.' 'I've got to present the results to the senior team.' The research presentation. The analyst presentation. The cleaners probably have a presentation too.

The danger with presentations is that you spend 90 per cent of the time constructing slides instead of thinking about how people might actually be influenced. We become consumed with the means, not the end. Rather than offering possibilities, we end up presenting presentations.

Most 'presentations' are actually saying 'Here is a workable possibility. We should talk about this.' If they don't say this, they are offering very little scope for influence.

“executives use PowerPoint like drunks use the edge of the bar. It props them up when they’re feeling uneasy about the world”

PITSTOP **PowerPoint**

I can’t work out if PowerPoint is great or something cooked up by Satan on one of his ‘let’s coop up the world in senseless exchanges while I get busy undoing civilization’ kicks.

Executives use PowerPoint like drunks use the edge of the bar. It props them up when they’re feeling uneasy about the world.

If Churchill had been brought up in this era, he’d have fired up his laptop and a slide would have appeared with:

My offer

- blood
- sweat
- tears

I don’t expect to wean you off your addiction to this thing, but try this next time. Use it to show pictures, graphs and nothing else. PowerPoint is really good for that.

No words. You do the words. That’s what your mouth is for.

Here’s a story about the email sent out by a newly installed boss of a software company in the US. I have it on good authority that this is true. If it is, this guy is my personal hero.

A quick note to let you know that I have just authorized the IT team to remove all PowerPoint software and presentations on our system. This has freed up 500 gigabytes of space, but more importantly, frees us up to talk with each other and our customers rather than present at one other. Please take the opportunity.

Best wishes
John

Issues to tackle

There are so many possible subjects for 'presentations' that I can't hope to anticipate your subject. What I can do is to offer a few tips to help you get your story straight.

What's the story?

This is the brutal question in the mind of anyone attending your session. There's no point in bringing them all together if you just have information to impart. That's what email is for.

You might be in sales, in audit, in service or project management, it doesn't matter. The job is the same. They are here to find out something that might just help them do their job better. You are there to give them that, or at the very least excite them about the possibility.

In the words of David Kean, one of my colleagues and a barnstorming salesman, 'You have to give them a sweetie.'

Do something unexpected

The unexpected means different things to different people. In a more sedate place like a bank, you may be making the point that your branch space needs to be organized differently to allow people to listen better to customers, and so you might change the way the chairs are arranged in the presentation room. In another company, you might want to talk about strong, direct actions for change, and remove both your shoes and bang them on a board director's head to make the point.

The classic example of this is the advertising agency who pitched for the British Rail account in the 1970s. The clients arrived at the plush London offices of the agency, but entered a reception area which was abandoned and unkempt. Staff wandered past occasionally, but responded brusquely to any requests for help or

Give them a sweetie

directions. After about half an hour, a crackly speaker announced 'Could the British Rail people come to conference room 2 on the first floor.' By now thoroughly irritated, the clients arrived at the conference room. 'Good morning', said the agency representative. 'This is how your customers feel.'

The point is momentarily to unbalance your listener. This creates the time, space and intrigue for you to influence.

Take authority

I'm grateful to Gareth Combes for teaching me this. When you give a 'presentation', you do people no favours if you fail to take authority. I don't mean strutting around like Mick Jagger on heat, but I do mean punching your weight in the room. The thing is that when people gather for a meeting and you take the floor, they *want* you to take authority for the next period of time. They are giving their time and attention and they'd like good use made of it. In fact, they get a bit freaked out if you don't. I imagine this goes back to the classroom, when, faced with a nervous or insecure teacher, we all started to misbehave without really knowing why.

So next time you stand up, remember this: they want to hear a story, and they want to hear it from you. They really do.

Example stories

Don't be afraid to use a story or two to allow your listeners to come on the journey with you. (Well, I would say that wouldn't I?) You can use them in several ways:

- to set the tone for the whole session
- to illustrate particular points
- to close, summarizing a particular argument.

Examples are legion, and the best are often ones you find yourself. However, here are a few that I've seen work to great effect. You can also choose from others in the trove in Appendix 1.

Customer service

A note in time . . .

At Raffles, in Singapore, a businessman who had never stayed there before was astonished by the way that people greeted him by name when he first checked in and went to his room. A sophisticated computer system or communication through headsets? No. What happens is that the cab driver writes a note of the guest's name, and passes it to the doorman just ahead of the customer, who passes it to the porter, who passes it to reception, who passes it back to the porter, who, after showing the guest to the room, passes it to the maid.

Joe's directions

At Four Seasons Hotels, they are famed for their attentiveness. A colleague of mine, who found herself lost and in the rain, driving towards the Washington DC hotel from Baltimore, called to get directions. The concierge was happy to help. No surprise there. What my colleague wasn't expecting was that Joe, having picked up the slightly frazzled tone of a stranger new to the city, stayed on the phone for 25 minutes to guide her in. 'Just to make sure ma'am.'

Getting the culture right

The Pret Experience Day

At Pret a Manger (more of them later), they believe that getting the right staff is critical to success. What they do, however, is let co-workers decide about new members of the teams. Apply to Pret and you'll go on a 'Pret Experience Day', where you work in-store for a day. You find out what it's about, and the people around you find out what it's like to work with you. At the end of the day (for which you're paid) your prospective colleagues vote, based on a clear set of criteria, as to whether you're the kind of person you and Pret customers would want to hang out with. Only one in ten make it. As the Chairman Andrew Rolfe says, 'If we trust people with our customers all day, we can surely trust them to make the right decision about who to hire to help them in that task.'

Power to the people

One of the most common calls to an electricity company is a query about the bill, or charging arrangements. One particular company had a complex system whereby there was a lot of this 'I'll have to speak to my manager' stuff for relatively small amounts.

A new service manager, with much head shaking from his colleagues, allowed each service operative much greater discretion, changing the amount they could negotiate with from £10 to an unlimited amount, covering the majority of calls. Result? The amount of money the company paid in settlements actually fell. The manager's case was proven – if you give people power, they won't abuse it, and the effect was actually to increase their sensitivity about the company's money.

Dinner time

One of the bosses at Chase Manhattan Retail in London tells of a lesson learned. 'I had this thing where if someone did

something outstanding, I'd pay for them to take out a partner for a good dinner with wine. The mistake I made was to put in the letter that there was a £100 limit on it. The average bill from these dinners was £110. When I stopped putting the bit about the £100 limit in the letter, the average bill dropped to £75. I think they were letting me know something, don't you?'

Quality

Be careful what you ask for . . .

An American company instructed their new Japanese supplier that the parts they had ordered should conform to the US firm's

exacting quality standards – 99.9 per cent conformity to specification. Confused, but determined to comply, the Japanese firm deliberately shipped one faulty component with every 999 perfect ones. A note accompanied the shipment stating that they were unsure why the customer wanted 0.1 per cent failure but were happy to oblige.

Interviews

You're probably grateful that I've got a lot less to say about job interviews. As an interviewee, I hate the process. As an interviewer, I normally end up feeling slightly insecure, as a succession of bright, talented and usually better-looking people troop up for the latest position in my organization.

Issues to tackle

Take authority

Yes, that one again. You're not there to justify yourself. Just as in the presentation, the interviewer will actually feel awkward if you don't take the lead. She's just come from another meeting, will have picked up your half-scanned CV from her groaning in-tray and is looking forward to being entertained for half an hour.

Have your story ready

An interviewer is looking for clues as to why you'll solve the problem they're facing. Normally, they'll be anxious about this problem, and therefore hiring becomes a largely irrational process. The best you can do is to be flexible in the moment, having prepared by the Law of Three.

1 What do you know about this person, the role and the organization?
2 What, explicitly, do you want them to think/do about you?
3 What story will help them step up to this?

The best question I was ever asked in an interview was 'What motivates you?' (It became quickly apparent that I wasn't at all sure.) The second best was this: 'Tell me about the crossroads you're at.' This was a rather elegant way of inviting me to tell my story, and, in doing so, make my pitch for the role. It also earned my interviewer time to get a sense of me and my priorities.

PITSTOP CVs/résumés

How did the CV become the paper currency of talent? And why are they all so dull? Tom Peters, the self-appointed Chief Deflater of Western Executive Ego (a job which needs doing) claims that we should reject CVs that don't have intriguing and unexplained gaps in them. And damn but he's right.

A CV is an opportunity to narrate your talent, not a reason to tabulate your career history. I especially hate the ones entitled 'Career Objective', followed by the usual witless nonsense about stretching yet fulfilling roles involving skills as blah blah . . .

In 15 years of reviewing CVs, I remember three. And I'm in the brand business, where you'd think people would have the first clue about marketing themselves. The first was done as a small, beautifully finished brochure about the person concerned. The second was pretty ordinary, but it arrived by Fedex, so you had to open it because you thought it would be important. The third was an intriguingly titled hyperlink to the person's website, which then had a little video of them.

Remember energy and fear. Don't let your fear (or your recruitment agency's fear) of being different get in the way of getting across your energy and story. Because that's what people want to hire.

> *we should reject CVs that don't have intriguing and unexplained gaps in them*

Success and failure

Failure to make it further in an interview process isn't a problem. I can't stress this enough. Failure is managing to get employed by a place that is substantially unsuited to you and you to them. A few years ago, we took on a young woman as a junior project manager, quiet, conscientious and willing. Then, in her second week, she just stopped turning up. We assumed illness, tried her mobile, got no response and eventually just assumed she'd given up on us. The following week we called her home (she lived with her parents, who were astonished). As far as they were concerned, she was still working with us. Every morning her mum packed her lunch, her dad dropped her off at the station, and every evening she told them about what had happened that day. In reality, she was just coming in to Victoria Station and wandering around all day. It breaks your heart, doesn't it?

Example stories

The people who are interviewing you will inevitably be making judgements about you – what you look like, what you sound like, what you say and how they feel about being around you. They need a couple of vivid hooks that will keep you in their memory, and for the right reasons. The right story can help to make that happen.

Your story is as personal as you. So rather than offer a selection of guesses, let's look at some of the low and high points of your career. Knowing what you *don't* want is as important as knowing what you do want. Sit down and let's look at some moments of truth.

What you dreamed of doing as a youngster

This is a really important clue. Not so much in the actual job as what it represents, or the skills it might entail. As a youngster, my dream was to be a hotel manager. Under that was actually my real career driver, which is to create experiences for people that make them feel good. I just happen to do it in a different sphere now. A friend of a friend always wanted to be a doctor, and is now a personal trainer at the local gym. It's the same thing, she says. I'm helping people get their bodies right – healing in another way.

I once met a very sophisticated young interviewee who explained how her childhood day-dream of being a tabloid reporter had evolved into being a communications professional. It was a compelling story.

The experience of your first or early job

The choice of your first job is usually fateful. Picasso once said that every painting is a recovery from the first stroke. Well, every career is a recovery from the first job.

What was it like? (What *is* it like, if you're doing it just now?) What do you remember about the interview, the selection process, the first few weeks? This is from a memorable conversation I had with a young guy who'd just come out of the army after completing five years.

I was freaked out by my first few weeks' training, I have to say. There was all the usual stuff, getting used to authority and getting your body strung out. But what really challenged me at first was the idea, the practice, of being responsible to others. After the line of authority, that's the most important thing in the army: you look out for one another, because if you don't, you're dead. It's symbolized by the practice of never leaving an injured soldier

"Picasso once said that every painting is a recovery from the first stroke. Well, every career is a recovery from the first job"

behind – so we ended up carrying each other quite a lot! Now, I expect I wouldn't face that here in an office – but the principle is the same. You just don't let people down, and when they need carrying, you carry them.

Did we hire that guy as a team leader for an established but under-performing group? I think so.

Now the armed forces always have that edge of glamour with which most of us can't compete. But other early work or professional experiences can serve you well. Whether it was a supermarket, office or factory, it's the same. You can express a key skill – service, teamwork, leadership, handling a crisis – by vivid reference to something that's happened to you in your early years and how you learned from it.

I've also heard a similar theme from people who've been involved in other group activities where you depend on one another – sailing, rowing or even theatre. If you can dramatize a particular skill or ability you have by creating a powerful story, you'll be remembered.

Moving jobs for the first time (if you did)

For a lot of us, moving jobs is one of the first adult decisions we make. The conveyor belt of school, college and interview rounds take us into the apparently grown-up world of our first 'proper' job. Now, equipped with the knowledge that (a) You want to progress and round out your skills or (b) You want to break down the nearest door marked EXIT, it's time to move on.

“if you can dramatize a particular skill or ability you have by creating a powerful story, you’ll be remembered”

This is often a time when you’re exploring what your professional story might be: what your energy is for, and where some of your fear lies, and how those two work together. This is good material for a story, and an opportunity to let your interviewer understand what really drives you.

In my early twenties, I left a job with a beer company based in Edinburgh. Beer is a great business to be in, and Edinburgh is a fantastic town. But I just couldn’t get up for the job, which was to be the brand manager of a new lager we had just launched. To do that job, you have to be single-mindedly dedicated to everything about that lager – you spend eight hours a day talking it up and negotiating on its behalf. And I discovered I’m not very single-minded. I’m several minded, which has its advantages as a consultant or adviser, because you can pull from lots of different ideas and sources to help a client get to a solution (Energy). But it makes me pretty useless at things that need dedication and consistency over long periods of time (Fear) Like putting up shelves, for example.

Formative moments or memories

This is a catch-all category, because there are incidents and narratives in all our working lives that define who we are and what we value.

There is a world of difference between banging on in abstract terms about what’s important to you and describing this in a vivid way so that someone can connect with you. Remember the universal law on page 10.

connection = stimulus + response

You provide the stimulus, and, provided it's set up for them and they've not been recently lobotomized, your listener will provide the response.

Boss/mentor tales

Describing a piece of wisdom learned from another can be effective. It shows you respect people (your interviewer may well be your next boss) and that you can learn without being arrogant about it.

A quote/suggestion of a business guru

Again, carefully handled, and leading to an observation or theory about the business you're trying to get into, this can work well. Not only are you showing an impressive breadth of reading, but it's odds on your interviewer

1 won't have read the idea, or

2 will have long forgotten it

and will therefore experience that unsettling yet disarming feeling of someone who knows more than you wanting to join your organization.

Summary

This chapter has been about the application of stories in two common business situations: presentations and interviews. In both, we've looked at the importance of understanding your audience, selecting stories to help them step up to what you want them to do, and providing them with vivid, memorable hooks that make your case. Good luck in your next encounter.

You and your business story

He who has the best story takes home the marbles.

Tom Peters

Making a living or heeding a call?

In Act 2 of this book, we're going to do a little work to explore your personal story. When I started to write this book, I didn't intend to spend more than ten pages on it. It was going to be about how you tell the story of your venture, your business, your project. But it became blindingly obvious to me that the two – your personal and business stories – are inseparable. Each forms part of the other.

For most people in more privileged countries, there is a great deal of intention in what we choose to do to make a living. We are called to certain jobs, roles or companies, even if we're not conscious of the fact.

Here are some email and live comments on this phenomenon.

> *your personal and business stories are inseparable: each forms part of the other*

Being called to a company or organization

'I only realized, I think, after several years, why I worked at this terminally frustrating but thoroughly enjoyable place. The company was founded by two strong-minded people, who each had clear, distinct roles. I, along with a few others, were, in practice, the big sisters and brothers of the family they had created. We 'managed' Mum and Dad, but sought their recognition, and looked after all the little ones when they weren't around. And it was the funniest thing to learn that virtually all of us in this second rank were the oldest child in our families!'

'I've jumped from job to job so many times now. I love the fix of being wanted by another person or organization, and leaving the frustration of something else behind.'

Being called to a role

'I think an artist has the closest overlap between who they are and what they do. The singer or actor gives of themselves – it's their source of emotional truth and therefore how "real" they feel to an audience.'

'Most people think I'm daft when I tell them this, but being an insurance salesman is absolutely the perfect job for me. You see, I really believe that protecting yourself against fate is a smart thing to do – I always have. This is a fantastic service for people, which is what keeps me going on a wet winter's night trying to find an appointment on some housing estate.'

'I'm a volunteer worker in a church, and my story is completely tied up in the story of Christ and his kingdom. Things changed for me a few years ago when I realized that if the story of Jesus, his resurrection and his message for the world is true, then it's the only thing that really matters. That's a powerful incentive!'

“the more your active value in life coincides with your active value in work, then the more chance of success you have. In both”

‘I’m a business consultant to medium-sized companies. I’ve spent most of my working life in larger companies, getting frustrated at how complicated they manage to make life for themselves and their customers. So my work is devoted to helping managers make things as simple as they can be, so that their energies are available for marketing and improving the business.’

The more your energy in life coincides with your energy in work, then the more chance of success you have. In both.

Think about the people you know who appear most fulfilled in what they do. Invariably, there will be a strong overlap between their personal enthusiasms and what they do for a living.

Telling the story of your venture

I may be accused of being oversimplistic, but I reckon most new ventures, projects, businesses or organizations need to answer only three questions: what’s the need for this, what’s the solution and why you?

So:
Rule 1 The need you are fulfilling (the market story)
Rule 2 How you fulfil the need (the product story)
Rule 3 Why you and no one else (the management/people story)

> *if this brand/product/service didn't exist, what would anyone miss?*

Rule 1 The need you are fulfilling (the market story)

When I was a young market researcher running focus groups, one of the most revealing questions was always this: *If this brand/product/service didn't exist, what would anyone miss?* Quite often people would say, 'well, nothing really', which was an interesting finding, except for those whose next promotion depended on the product in question.

Your task here is to find a compelling way of describing the market need, and this is often best done through story. One of my all-time favourites is the founding story of Innocence Drinks. Here's their story, in their words.

In the summer of 1998 when we had developed our first smoothie recipes but were still nervous about giving up our proper jobs, we bought £500 worth of fruit, turned it into smoothies and sold them from a stall at a little music festival in London. We put up a big sign saying 'Do you think we should give up our jobs to make these smoothies?' and put out a bin saying 'YES' and a bin saying 'NO' and asked people to put the empty bottle in the right bin. At the end of the weekend the 'YES' bin was full so we went in the next day and resigned.

Notice how the story combines a vivid image of demand (the full YES bin) with the sense of personal risk that the founders were taking – and their belief in getting people to drink healthier, tastier drinks and have a good time doing so. (A little like, in a different market, what they say at a certain brewery. 'Drink a bit of Guinness, make a bit of money, have a bit of fun.')

“the art here is to find an anchor point for your audience”

Your story can be less lyrical, but equally strong.

Often they have different angles:

This Is Just Stupid, Folks
Why does this product range have fourteen different types of tension screw when three would do? (Quality team to industry consortium)

People Shouldn't Have To Put Up With This
We think the people of London shouldn't have to put up with badly made and worse tasting sandwiches in their lunch hour. (Pret A Manger)

Things Can Be Better
You ought to have 24-hour access to your bank, with nice people at the end of the line. (first direct)

Flying ought to be cheaper and universally available. (Easyjet)

The art here is to find an anchor point for your audience. There is an almost childlike simplicity to the best of the market stories, which is precisely why they are so strong.

Rule 2 How you fulfil the need (the product story)

Okay, let's take this a little further with the help of our friends at Pret A Manger. First, the market story is established. Every day in London, there are hundreds of thousands of people who are in a hurry, looking for great tasting sandwiches and deserve better than they're getting. So, how is this need to be fulfilled?

PITSTOP Why people really start companies

The business author Art Klein has written eloquently on what organizations are for. They're not, he says, to meet market or public needs. They're there so that a small group of people, normally near the top of the organization, can have a really good time. They create or fashion places where they can exercise a sense of power, risk and enjoyment. They rest of us are there to help them have a good time, and, if we're lucky, we might as well.

'Do you know why I run this company?' said the Chairman of a consultancy, after an excellent lunch. 'It's part of a lifetime's campaign to end the underlining of phrases or words in documents. It disfigures much of modern society and I'm determined to root it out.'

This man was only partly joking. I include the story because I feel it's an entirely laudable aim, and certainly more important than the routine business of the company, which was advising young marketing guns on what the colour of their new crisp packets should be.

First, you put out your stall. These sandwiches are going to taste better because first, we use fresher, better ingredients, and second, we make them right here in the store every day, rather than bus them in from Northampton. Handmade, natural products.

This is rather clever, you see. Pret realized that people wanted quality and freshness, but that a lot of them didn't want to hang around watching their sandwiches be made (or more accurately, watch other people's being made as you waited behind them in a queue).

Put out your stall

The choice for a sandwich buyer was *either* go to Marks and get an okay sandwich pretty quickly *or* go to a sandwich bar where you could get something made up for you, and flirt with members of the extended Italian or Greek family running the joint, *“great product stories are those which resolve the either/or dilemma in a market, and say, fine, have both”*

which ended up taking half your lunch hour. Pret A Manger said that you can have your cake (and your sandwich), and eat it. A freshly made, really tasty sandwich in an environment built for speed. And if you want to sit down and eat it, that's cool too. The coffee is better than the stuff that passes for cappuccino in most sandwich bars.

Essentially, great product stories are those which resolve the either/or dilemma in a market, and say, fine, have both. Examples would be:

Foo Fighters	Edgy guitar rock *and* brilliant tunes
Ikea	Quality furniture *and* it's affordable
Amazon.com	Amazing choice *and* almost impossibly convenient
Malmaison Hotels	Chic *and* in city centres where the business is
Harley Davidson	Performance *and* impeccable cool *

The key thing for the market story is to anchor the need. The key thing for the product story is to narrate how what you do fulfils the need.

Rule 3 Why you and no one else (the people story)

The only venture capitalist I know says that his team makes decisions partly on the soundness of the business idea but mostly on the capability of the management team.

* As someone from Harley once said, if you are a 50-year-old accountant, this brand is the one chance you have of turning up in a small town and people feeling scared of you.

“to investors, partners, customers, the thing is this – why you guys?”

To investors, partners, customers, the thing is this – why you guys? Especially if you haven’t got a unique or compelling service offer, you’re going to have to convince people you’re the right people for the job. I don’t know all the qualities you need, but what I do know is that you have to describe them in a way that captures attention.

Back to our friends at Pret.

We’re just very, very passionate about the things we care about.

Andrew Rolfe, Chairman and CEO, Pret A Manger

Pret had a pretty good business idea. But, then again, lots of people have that. Their ability was to make their character – up, passionate, delighting in service and good food – an essential part of who they were as a business.

Here’s part of a pitch document I saw recently from a start-up consulting business:

‘We’ve spent the best part of 20 years consulting to big companies and senior people. We don’t want to do it anymore. We just want to work on small-scale projects or with small businesses. We don’t want to work with Non Value Adding Departments. NVADs are everywhere in big companies, and normally above the fourth floor. They are stuffed with bright, and for the most part, pleasant people, who contribute nothing to the business of the business except the occasional web site. We’re a small business, working for small fees, for small businesses. Because that’s the way we like it, and, we suspect, you will too.’

That strikes me as a brilliant bit of market positioning, but above all, it speaks to the quality of focus and passion of the people concerned. The people who started this business probably always wanted to make a difference to the companies they worked with: they believed in using their minds and energy to help companies get better. Now they've come up against Nemesis – the Non Value Adding Departments who get in the way of their belief. So, in a neat sidestep, they're saying that in order to preserve their belief, they will work only with smaller businesses. This is a commercial risk, but it comes from the heart, just like saying that we will make only handmade, natural food. It is a choice. And choices make stories.

To conclude this chapter, let's just review what we've learned, referencing the Pret story. They'd better give me a free coffee next time I'm in, I'll tell you.

- You need a *market story*: a way of anchoring the need. (There are too many Londoners eating sub-standard lunches.)
- You need a *product story*: how you fill that need. (Natural, handmade products, with you at speed in a friendly environment.)
- You need a *people story*: how only you can do this. (We are more passionate and committed to this than you can imagine, and that flows through every one of our stores.)

So, whatever your business, project or venture, get your story straight. And take home the marbles.

5

Finding a story and making it your own

Where we look at a real-life example of using story to encourage change in a business

Making connections

I'm writing this high above America. America's got a Big Sky. I've spent most of the flight marvelling at how easy the pilots, engineers and crew make such a trip. And right now, I'm in a silent rapture at the idea of eating a Cornish clotted cream tea 30,000 feet above the Atlantic seaboard in a small tube bulleting towards a city in the West.

Ahead lie a series of meetings at which I'm going to try to make connections. I've been asked to provide consulting support to our US colleagues as they work with a new client, a large financial business. I spend the flight reading some of the initial papers.

Like many banks, this one is waking up to the potential of its brand as a symbol of what it wants to do for people. (Or, as cynics might have it, what it wants to do to people.)

“if your brand is clear enough, then everyone gets the picture”

The documents are perceptive and thorough. They describe the intent of the business to serve its customers by providing an enduring, insightful relationship. (I think they mean by this that if you know someone better, you can serve them and sell to them better.) The bank would like this quality to show up reliably in contact with customers, in advertising and communication, and in the ‘contract’ they seek to build with their employees.

Now, companies and organizations have always sought ways of trying to provide some focus, so that when people ask ‘What’s this company for, or what does it do for me?’ the CEO has a fighting chance of making a decent reply. Most organizations, incidentally, fail this basic test.

A parent took her 5-year-old to the theatre. The show featured a rather laboured actor, who got particular attention from her son. After an hour of puzzling, he turned to his mum, and in a none too discreet whisper, said ‘Mummy, what is that man for?’

The most recent, and arguably effective way of providing a compass for the organization is to use its brand. At best, this brand is a symbol for a distinctive set of activities that are of practical and emotional use to people. For example, Burger King is a symbol of the promise of hot, halfway tasty food for people on a timetable. You know where you stand with Burger King, as presumably do the people behind the till who cook and serve at a roaring pace so that you can get on with your day.

If your brand is clear enough, then everyone gets the picture. The hard part is getting to this simplicity.

At the bank, the meetings have a peculiar flavour. They are intent, cynical and jovial in turn. For me, there is a suspended *“multi platform connectivity is one of those lovely examples of what is technically known as a crap phrase”*

sense of reality. The conversation is meant to be about how we can connect the 30,000 employees of a bank to the idea behind the bank. Yet the language in the room is far from connecting. People speak from behind the walls of their particular function. They clam up when anyone more senior speaks, even if they speak nonsense.

We get to the strategy – the idea we want people to understand. What is it? What is it that we want people in the bank to get up for?

It turns out to be something called Multi Platform Connectivity.

Oh God.

I end up mildly unpopular by persistently trying to question what this means. It turns out that it means teaming up across the business units to sell services to customers who might otherwise go outside the bank for them. (For example, referring a current account holder who needs motor insurance to the insurance business unit.)

A long discussion ensues about Multi Platform Connectivity. During it, someone mentions the following. The Chief Executive had been conducting one of his regular, all employee conference calls (anyone can just dial into the conversation) and was trying to get across this concept. A memorable response was from a mortgage guy somewhere in Allentown, Pennsylvania. He asked, rather plaintively, ‘So who do I call up to do this multi connecting stuff?’

And right there was the clue we were looking for. A story, imperfectly formed, shone out of the fog. It was the authentic voice of

PIT*STOP* Jargon

Multi Platform Connectivity is one of those lovely examples of what is technically known as a Crap Phrase. You get these all the time at senior management levels. People start using words and phrases because they appear to confer dignity and strength on the user, while merely disguising their terror at the job facing them. It's like chefs who put 'sauce anglaise' on the menu because 'custard' is beneath them.

Crap phrases that litter business:

Crap phrase	Used by senior executive because
Mission	Everyone in all those case studies has a mission, don't they? Disney? Tom Cruise?
Strategic priorities	'The things we've go to do' doesn't have that presidential ring about it, does it?
Leadership competencies	We need a list of things to mark people on. Especially people who might be after my job.
Leverage	It makes me feel like there are actually some levers I can pull
Strategy	Our set of rough guesses about the future
Portfolio	The rats' nest that is our business
Strategic business units	The main rats

Place little trust in people who use these words or phrases, especially if they attempt to use two in one sentence.

the bank, perplexed and well-meaning. So how do I do this stuff? This was how we could connect a piece of management garbage (MPC) with the idea of the bank.

The story could be used as a catalyst in at least a couple of ways. The first is to tell it as it happened in this instance, and bring to mind the needs of the bank employees for pragmatic guidance and help. The story makes plain the gap between the high language and ideals of MPC and the reality of delivering it. With this established in the audience's mind, the teller can then draw out the implications.

Another way would be to retell the story by finding a positive model, smuggling in the change idea you want to communicate and letting people's minds work on that. It was the matter of a few phone calls to uncover a mortgage salesperson who had used her wit and a connection to refer someone to another part of the bank for a pension. Her name was Marci Allen, and we had ourselves a protagonist.

Marci's story

In September 2001, Marci Allen, a mortgage adviser in Buffalo, was helping a client with a re-mortgage for their family home. During the financial check-up, she established that the family didn't have adequate pension provision – and that she wasn't sure how to advise them.

She had the business card of a financial planning colleague somewhere in her handbag. They'd met at a get-together two months back and had really got on. She called the number and was able to hand the customer a phone with a friendly voice on the end of the line.

The client ended up with a great mortgage deal, a personal pension with the bank, and the sense that things had been connected up for them. All because two people had got on and exchanged business cards.

In finding Marci's story, we found an important, but overlooked ingredient. All sensible banks have numbers you call if you want to cross-refer customers. But behind those numbers are people you don't know. And how inclined do you feel to cross-refer your customers to people you don't know? Customer service and salespeople are driven by getting things done for the person in front of them. Their energy tends to be about delivering things for people. Their fear tends to be about letting people down. Handing someone over (or Multi Platform Connectivity) involves the risk of letting somebody down.

Mostly, we like to do business with someone, not with something. That applies as much inside an organization as between customer and supplier. The whole success of the bank's strategy lay in the thousand equivalents of Marci handing over the phone.

Marci's version of Multi Platform Connectivity was that she had met a specialist with whom she got on with and reckoned she could trust. The key to 'MPC' was not orders or a better intranet, it was better relationships within the bank. You have to know someone before you'll hand over a customer. Let's re-look at the story.

	Set up
In September 2001, Marci Allen, a mortgage adviser in Buffalo, was helping a client with a re-mortgage for their family home.	Preps the audience for the story's relevance and introduces the protagonist
During the financial check-up, she established that the family didn't have adequate pension provision – and that she wasn't sure how to advise them.	**Beginning** **The predicament or crisis** facing our hero – which is imaginable for the audience
She had the business card of a financial planning colleague somewhere in her handbag. They'd met at a get-together two months back and had really got on. She called the number and was able to hand the customer a phone with a friendly voice on the end of the line.	**Middle** **The predicament is resolved by** a choice and course of action and struggle. The action reflects the main theme of making connections for customers
The client ended up with a great mortgage deal, a personal pension with the bank, and the sense that things had been connected up for them. All because two people had got on and exchanged business cards.	**End** **The result** of the activity – reflecting the audience's concern and / or the change idea. Drawing out of implications.

Marci's story is the start of a real conversation about the idea of the bank.

I hope Act 1 of the book has spoken to you. I wanted to provide a set of ideas and tools to help you influence for good. Next up, we're going to look at your personal story, and the important bearing it has on you as a professional.

act 2

The story of your life

6

What's the story?

In which we discover whether you're living in a briefcase or out of a rucksack, what a protagonist is and why you're one

When you stop taking risks, well that's the end of the story.

Oliver Stone

Snapshot

The London Underground has a branch called the Piccadilly Line. The western part of the line runs between Heathrow Airport and central London. If you get on about 7.30 on a weekday morning, travelling towards town, you'll see two sorts of people. There are people with briefcases on their daily commute into the city. And there are people with rucksacks, folks of all ages just off the overnight flights from Australia, the US, South America.

And you can imagine the difference. One group is enduring the journey. The other is relishing it. Strap hanging, I listen in, as you do. Two young Kiwi women, hair pulled back, try to figure out their immediate plans – where they're going to stay, how they're going to fix up temporary jobs, who they're going to pull strings with. They're on their way.

From behind their papers, the regular commuters hear this. Many think 'good on them'. Some think 'if only'. Some have long since stopped listening.

We're all of us on a journey. Since none of us can know with any certainty how it will end, there's only really one topic for debate – how we choose to travel.

Is it going to be in a briefcase or out of a rucksack?

The choice is an important one. Glance at the table below and see what your journey currently feels like.

Do you want a briefcase story?	Or do you want a rucksack story?
A bit numb a lot of the time	A taste for the business of life
Emotionally closed	Emotionally open
Avoiding risks	Up for some risk
Shirking choices	Facing up to choices
Deflecting responsibility	Owning responsibility
Life as a diary	Life as a drama
A bit dull, frankly	Cool to listen to

1. If you're spending a lot of the time in the left-hand column and are happy there, you should stop now because the next section will just annoy you.
2. If you're spending a lot of time in the left and don't much care for it, steam ahead.
3. If you're mostly in the right-hand column, good on you, but stick around, because there's a bunch of things here to help you keep you there.

(Oh and for those of you who are thinking, 'Hang on, he's stopped talking about business,' well I haven't.)

This book has a simple proposition. You owe it to yourself to strap on a rucksack.

In order to help you do this, we're going to work out the answer to a fairly sizeable question: What's *your* story?

Your story is simply what's important to you, the choices you've made and risks you've taken in pursuit of what's important, and where all that is now taking you. Most importantly, your story is the energy and fear inside you.

Slip on your rucksack

> *“to influence people, you need to know what influences you”*

This is a book about influencing people. To influence people, you need to know what influences *you*.

In Act 1 we looked at influence: how you use the craft of stories to tell your business story and take others with you. In Act 2 we're going to look at what an interesting story needs. We're going to learn from movies and we're going to learn from organizations. We're going to help you put together where you've been, what you do and where you're headed.

Prepare to slip on your rucksack.

Questions for protagonists

A protoganist in a script carries the meaning of the film. The question here is what meaning are *you* carrying? What beliefs are you trying to enact in your life? What's driving your drama?

I remember going to a job interview ten years ago. The guy interviewing me didn't bother with all the gunk about my education and experience. He just looked me in the eye and said: 'Iain, what motivates you? I'd really like to know what motivates you?' I did a passable impression of a goldfish and failed the interview.

Over recent months. I've been asking a range of people the same question. There's a staggering variety of answers:

- Providing for my family
- Doing Allah's will
- Enjoying as much as I can while I'm still young enough

- Solving my clients' problems
- Getting through the day
- I haven't the faintest idea

All are legitimate answers. Look hard enough and you can see the human drama behind each of them.

Now, QFP time (Questions for Protagonists). Try these. Note down your answers if you like. I've filled in mine, in a rare moment of candour (as sample responses).

I am motivated by...
(a dream, a belief, an obligation, a cheque, whatever it is in your life that you believe endures)
Sample response:
A belief in that people can find their energy and so realize more of themselves.

You can tell this because ....
(examples of the way you act, the choices you make, the evidence you have – stuff someone else could understand)
Sample response:
I help people in business give voice to who they are and what they want to do. I'm writing this book. I spend regular time with my children to help them express themselves.

The main conflict in my life is.......................................
(Between you and someone else? Within your head? Between your motivation – see above – and external circumstances? Remember if there's no conflict, there's no story.)
Sample response:
There are a couple. Between freedom and security. Between my need to play, goof off and fantasize, and my need to provide for those I love and contribute to the lives of others. There is also another. Between my sense of our collective human dignity and circumstances that tarnish that dignity. In my professional life, this is most often evident in the incessant

and clueless drive for economic growth. Life, for many of us, is an effort to preserve dignity in the face of the dollar.

What do I long to do?..

(Funny word, 'long', isn't it? What sounds distant is probably right round the corner, were we just to look.)

Sample response:

I long to spend my life working with others so that, together, we feel more energy and expression in our lives. Oh, and earn a living doing so.

Try it out. If the results don't feel satisfactory to you, try this little tip. Ask 'Why?' If you say that power motivates you, ask 'Why?' Then ask it again. Eventually you come to what you're actually batting for.

7

When Stuff Happens

What to do when you're thrown off balance, and why *American Beauty* was such a hit

When Stuff Happens

What I like about the story form is that, like life, it embraces the fact that Stuff Happens to you. It doesn't pretend life is like one of these You Can Create The Life You Always Wanted To This Weekend audio tapes. (I should know, I've got several.)

The thing about a story is that it is often external circumstances (Stuff) that force the main character to make a choice about what they long to do. In *Erin Brockovich*, Erin is involved in a car accident which throws her together with a legal system that eventually becomes the stage for her fulfilment.

In a story, a character is thrown off balance, and they have to make a choice about what to do. That choice entails risk. It gets progressively more risky. If it didn't, we'd stop listening or watching. In *The Shawshank Redemption*, the abuse that Andy Dufresne receives at the hands of warders and inmates sends him in a tailspin. He makes a choice – to set up his own escape *“story is trying to tell us something. It's trying to tell us what to do when stuff happens”*

and to civilize some aspects of the regime. He makes this choice even though it would be easier to avoid it.

Screenwriters call Stuff 'the forces of antagonism' (protagonists face antagonists, if you see) which I always think has a nice grand ring to it. It is in facing these forces that character is revealed, in its misery or glory.

Story is trying to tell us something. It's trying to tell us what to do when Stuff Happens.

Here's the daily business of life. Things are chugging along reasonably well, when Stuff Happens. This could range from getting caught in traffic to being made redundant.

1 Stuff happens (at work, in personal life, in the street, wherever) @**& (expletive of your choice). *Life is just one damn thing after another*.

2 Then:

either 2A Who can I blame or moan to? Or what can I drink?

or 2B Maybe I could make a choice about how I respond to this.

We all go through Stage 1, unless you're Spock, the Dalai Lama or someone who's read *The Seven Habits of Highly Effective People*. They skip straight to 2B.

Most of us jump into the swamps of 2A, since we've been successfully shifting responsibility for things since we were 4 years old and realized we could get our baby sister to take the rap for that broken window.

Most of us stay right here, replaying the first act of a stillborn story.

Some lucky people make it to the uplands of 2B – rolling with the punch and figuring out the next move.

And if you hang out in the uplands long enough, you come to a startling realization (I jolted in my chair writing this): **When stuff happens, it's part of my story**. Not anyone else's. It's not some giant cosmic game with me as the pawn. It's a new act in who I am and where I'm going. And this Stuff is actually what makes my story interesting.

Cinematically, one of the most successful stories of all time is *Star Wars*. At its heart is a simple conflict: Light, in the person of Luke Skywalker, and Darkness, in the cloak of Darth Vader. Throw in the fact that Darkness is also Daddy and you have a winner. Without Daddy-Darth, you'd just have a good-looking lad with laser sword romping around carving up robots. No antagonism.*

PITSTOP African resistance fighter

Ask nothing.
Blame no one.
Do something.

Steve Biko

I can't stress this too strongly. It's in meeting the forces of antagonism that you switch on to what your story really is. I use the term deliberately. When a story bores us, we switch the TV off

---

*Another variation on My Father Is The Antichrist is *The Devil's Advocate*. This isn't much of a film and I'm only mentioning it because Al Pacino's a great demon and because of the moment where Keanu Reaves (the son) discovers the awful truth.

Keanu: You're, you're the devil?

Al: Call me Dad!

or close the book. When a person bores us, we switch off. (Be honest now.)

When you bore you, you get switched off. You may even shut down.

Next thing you know, you're sitting on the Underground listening to other people making travel plans.

When we reach the gates, God doesn't look us over for medals. He looks us over for scars.

Anon

Smart guy, that Anon.

A case study in finding your story: *American Beauty*

Death is like a freight train in the future, heading towards us, closing the hours second by second, between now and then. If we're to live with any sense of satisfaction, we must engage life's forces of antagonism before the train arrives.

Robert McKee

I wonder how many of us feel like Lester Burnham at the beginning of *American Beauty*? He's living a briefcase life. He feels numb. Things are in monochrome, not colour.

The story of *American Beauty* is his rediscovery of wonder. For a few months, he rediscovers that life is to be relished, not endured. That risk enhances, not diminishes life.

Lester is a man who has lost his way. Here's Lester starting his day. His voice-over provides a knowing counterpoint.

“Lester is a man who has lost his way”

Lester (V.O.) (*amused*) Look at me, jerking off in the shower. (*then*) This will be the high point of my day. It's all downhill from here.

It's a pathetic sight. In fact, that's the one thing that everyone agrees on at the start of *American Beauty*: Lester is pathetic.

He has lost his story, lost his truth, and in doing so, has earned the contempt of those closest to him – his wife Carolyn and daughter Jane. They sense only a presence in the house, that whatever was vital about this man long since departed. Only we, the viewers, share his own mordant understanding about what is going on.

Lester (V.O.) I have lost something. I'm not exactly sure what it is, but I know I didn't always feel this . . . sedated. But you know what? It's never too late to get it back.

There is a bright spot somewhere in Lester's mind, of which he speaks halfway through the film. It was a time before the weight of obligation and convention descended. When he flipped burgers, chased girls and drove a Pontiac Firebird. When he felt like a man.

The brilliance of the structure of this film is that the one certainty of life, death, is introduced up front. The first scene shows Lester's daughter, only half-jokingly, asking someone to kill her father. The second scene introduces Lester, and the fact that he's going to die pretty soon.

We're FLYING above suburban America, DESCENDING SLOWLY toward a tree-lined street.

Lester (V.O.) My name is Lester Burnham. This is my neighborhood. This is my street. This . . . is my life. I'm 42 years old. In less than a year, I'll be dead.

Of course, I don't know that yet.

He rolls over, looks up at us and sighs. He doesn't seem too thrilled at the prospect of a new day.

Lester (V.O.) (*cont'd*) And in a way, I'm dead already.

The basic questions of life are deftly introduced.

1 The only certain thing about life is death.
2 When death happens is uncertain.
3 Given this, how are you going to live your life?

The film tells you death is going to happen and soon. So how is Lester going to live his life? You're hooked.

Lester's life is everything we talked about a minute ago. His life bores him. He bores other people. He bores himself.

Gradually, Stuff Happens. A series of events conspire to shift Lester. A set of choices confront him. In making these choices, he recaptures what it is to feel alive.

Let's look at them. Every one, I promise you, has a counterpoint in your own life.

Stuff Happens	What Lester would normally do	What he does
He is asked to reapply for his own job – a thinly disguised exercise in making him redundant.	Beg or plead for another change. Try and reapply.	Uses insider knowledge (a senior executive's abuse of expenses) to negotiate a year's severance pay. He then takes a job in a burger bar.
He meets one of his daughter's friends who he finds stunningly attractive.	Masturbate in the shower.	Pursues her, flirts with her, and starts a regime of physical fitness to try and impress her.

At an evening drinks party, his wife flirts with a male business associate	Get drunk.	Goes outside and gets stoned with a waiter, who turns out to be his next door neighbour and a convenient source of pot.

Whatever you feel about Lester's actions, they are all in pursuit of his truth – to re-discover the sense of vitality and wonder of life that he feels has been lost. Life, at last, has a bite to it, and that is more mind-enhancing than all the dope he's now smoking.

In the rest of the film, the risks build on themselves. Lester makes a series of choices, gradually upping the ante as he revises his expectations of what life should be about. This goes on to the end of the line, to a final action beyond which we cannot imagine another – his murder. And, ironically, the murder is committed by his neighbour, a man who has choked up all his sexuality, passion and shame. He can only release it by killing someone who has achieved what he longs for.

The last thing we see of Lester is him sitting at the kitchen table, a look of almost incandescent wonder on his face. He has awoken, only moments before he is to die.

These are the film's closing words.

Lester (V.O.) I guess I could be pretty pissed off about what happened to me . . . but it's hard to stay mad, when there's so much beauty in the world. Sometimes I feel like I'm seeing it all at once, and it's too much, my heart fills up like a balloon that's about to burst . . .

. . . and then I remember to relax, and stop trying to hold on to it, and then it flows through me like rain and I can't feel anything but gratitude for every single moment of my stupid little life . . . (*amused*) You have no idea what I'm talking about, I'm sure. But don't worry . . .

“stories are about what endures, despite change”

FADE TO BLACK

Lester (V.O.) *(cont’d)* You will someday.

Where have we got so far?

1. Stories are about what endures, despite change. They tell us about a belief or value that is worth standing for. In Lester’s case, it’s vitality and wonder.
2. Most of us are unaware of our own story. We’re playing the extras in someone else’s drama. This is the world of the briefcase.
3. If you’re not switched on to your story, you may end up losing interest in your life and yourself. Remember Lester: *‘In a way, I’m dead already.’*
4. Stories thrive in conflict and antagonism. The choices you make, the action you take under pressure, reveal what you stand for.
5. Once you do this, you become a protagonist. You stand for something bigger and better than your own self-interest. You can look yourself in the mirror again. And see that rucksack peeping over your shoulder.

Let’s pack for the journey.

8

Your story

In which we discover the delight and danger of *your* story

The elements

Why must we write from the inside out? What do we gain if we do? What do we sacrifice if we don't? The only reliable source of emotional truth is yourself.

Robert McKee

Every story holds a promise. It's a promise that will be tested in the telling.

Think of last night's TV. Think Phil, Deirdre, Morse, Homer. All characters, or protagonists, whose promise to you, their audience, is that they will search for their truth.

Stories are containers. They are the basic form for creating meaning. Just as the cup on my desk contains coffee, so stories contain meaning. They exist to help you and I make sense of ourselves and the world.

“every story holds a promise”

One important function is to help us understand how time passes. The very sense of time passing is created by the form of a story. Listen in to any conversation between an adult and baby, and you'll hear a start, a little crescendo of mutual chatter, and close. One of the most frequent acts, the nappy change, becomes a mini epic. ('Off it comes, here's the wipe, look – another nappy! Fix it on, all done.')

Through thousands of these little narratives, we build a sense of past, present and future. The form of story is hardwired into us.

Another important function is to enable us to tell the story of our own lives. Of all the stories you tell, this is the most crucial to you. Your story.

You've probably pieced it together like this. As a child, you learned from adults, from anecdotes, from photographs, from listening in. You learned about your past, your place in the family, your gender, and the basic beliefs of the family or group to which you belonged.

As you grew up, you picked up a sense of your own skills and preferences, of what you liked and loved, of what you feared. In your young head, you juggled a set of meanings and created a basic set of beliefs about the world.

Watching, listening and talking to others older than you, to papers and TV, you tried out different futures. As a girlfriend or mother, father or lover, footballer or dancer, friend or scoundrel. You sifted these different ideas and tested them out. My five-year-old daughter's current plan is to become a fire-fighter and marry her friend Callum. Who knows? She might be right.

By the time you venture into the adult world, let's say at 16, you have to have a working story in place about yourself. (Of course, the basics are in place long before then, but I'm not qualified to talk about that. I have two small children and I'm buggered if I can understand what's going on with them.)

Having pieced together your story, it is tested by the outside world. Most of our adult lives are spent testing and adjusting our stories as new or unfamiliar conditions arise.

The delight and the danger

The delight of our story is that it helps us form a secure basis for venturing into the world and living with others. It offers a promise of what should happen in the future. The danger is that it will turn out to be substantially wrong in important respects.

Two of the most common myth-stories in the West are written for little girls and little boys. The first is Cinderella. In it, the promise is made that, should you be good, pretty, and maybe just a little flirty, Prince Charming will find, love you, and look after you for ever. (In the Sleeping Beauty variant, you just need to be pretty and patient and he'll eventually turn up. Hell, you can even doze off.) Two of the most successful films of recent times, *Pretty Woman* and *Bridget Jones's Diary*, are strikingly well-written updates of Cinderella.

The second takes many forms, which we'll call Action Man as shorthand. It is where a man or boy takes on special powers, defeats enemies and is rewarded with power, esteem or love. The runaway success of Harry Potter is the latest example in a long line. (David Beckham, Luke Skywalker, Aladdin, Robin Hood, Peter Pan, Mowgli . . .)

These are delightful, dangerous stories. They are powerful enough to keep us enchanted, long after the evidence of our adult life is that Prince Charmings are thin on the ground and that power, or its rewards, is illusory.

“one of the bittersweet joys of being human is that you are both the actor and the writer”

Their principal danger is that they promise a perfect future. And daily life tells us that life is imperfect and the future unknowable.

Your story is something you have written again and again. It is worn into your mind like the contours made by a river. But it is only a fiction. It won't be exactly as you predict. Or perhaps anything like it.

One of the bittersweet joys of being human is that you are both the actor and the writer. You are neither the blind follower of instructions ('I was only following orders') nor the detached author.

When I became a man, I put away childish things.

The Bible, somewhere

Stories for grown-ups

As an adult, you can rewrite your story. In fact, you probably have to, unless you're living in a bubble. This doesn't mean giving up what is important to you. It just means allowing for the fact that you, the world and the people around you are imperfect. And that your future will be imperfect too.

You know, sometimes I think the only world I'll be happy in is the world I make up.

Ally McBeal

I hate saying this. Believe me, I do. Part of me would like nothing more than to live out my adolescent fantasy of a life as a renowned musician (special powers), attracting a series of fragile beauties to my riverside penthouse (love), a web of friends

> *“our lives are a succession of conflicts and resolutions . . . more Ally McBeal than Cinderella”*

and admirers moved by my music and words (esteem/power). But it ain’t going to happen. Partly because it’s a bit ludicrous, but mostly because it’s isolating and unrewarding, which is the bit of the Action Man legend the stories aren’t big on.

Stories are satisfying because they deliver on the promise. They package up the ending and you’re left feeling complete. Harry defeats his demons. Bridget gets her man.

But if you’re stuck with a childlike story in an adult world, then it can be tough. Adult stories, real world stories, have a curious element to them. There is no big ending. No final resolution. (Apart from the freight train.) In fact, our lives are a succession of conflicts and resolutions, in which we play a part. In that, they are like a soap opera, rather than an epic. More Ally McBeal than Cinderella.

These events may be random, or they may have a theme. If there is no theme, no controlling idea, as a screenwriter would say, life will feel like an accident.

It’s your job to identify the theme. It’s your job to be the writer. Let’s try it together.

Writing your story

As a new writer on *EastEnders*, one of the first things you have to do is look at the ‘backstory’ of each of the characters you’ll be writing about. It’s all documented. Their parents, their affairs, their problems, their joys. In order to write about Cath or Phil you have to know where they came from.

Backstory is what has happened as you embark on the next part of your story. As the author of your own story, you need to know your own backstory.

First, let's make acquaintance with you on the threshold of adulthood. Imagine yourself sitting in a chair. Opposite you is an empty chair. Someone enters the room and sits in the chair. It is you aged 16.

What do you see? What is this person's body language?

How would this 16-year-old reply to the following questions? Please note this down in the book.

Who are you?

How are you?

What does your upbringing tell you is important?

What are your plans?

What do you love to do?

What or who do you love? Why?

What or who do you fear? Why?

What do you see in your future?

Using this, let's look at the story this 16-year old took into adulthood. We'll use the basic elements that a screenwriter would in building a story.

The theme

By 'theme' we mean the basic drive behind the story – the one-sentence summary of the story's meaning. Your story is either idealistic, pessimistic or ironic. Cinderella and Action Man are based on idealistic values. A hero or heroine, who, through a series of trials, is rewarded or something is restored. (Love will triumph, justice will be done.)

Equally, the theme may be pessimistic. (Life is or will be empty, passion will destroy you.) These stories don't tend to be big box office, unless in the hands of a master, like Mike Leigh, who creates compassion as people root around in the dustbin of their lives.

“a character is revealed in the choices made under pressure”

Somewhere in between are ironic themes. This is an idea charged with positive and negative. Rather than idealism or tragedy, the story voices both. It is redemptive – your obsession can destroy you, unless you realize it in time. Or it can be punitive – you reap the rewards of your obsession, then you are punished.

The theme requires an active value – something which you hold to be true and useful in your life.

What's the theme of your story at 16? What was the promise that life held?

It's important we get as clear as possible on this. If we're going to rewrite something, we'll need the original. Here are some examples.

Personal theme	Mostly
I will earn legitimacy and esteem from others. *Active value – achievement*	Idealistic
I will fly high and soar, but my wings will be . clipped *Active value – achievement*	Ironic
The right woman/man will make me happy. *Active value – being deserving of love*	Idealistic
I don't deserve love. *Active value – self-denial/cynicism*	Pessimistic
(variation on above) I mess up in love, but I'm a survivor. *Active value – adventuring*	Ironic
I'll be free to do whatever I want. *Active value – personal liberty*	Idealistic (ironic)

Write yours here:

My personal theme/active value	Mostly

Recognize that you have been in pursuit of this for as long as you can remember.

Character

A character is revealed in the choices made under pressure.

Thinking now as an adult, whatever your age is, what have you done, or what do you do, to ensure that the theme and active value are preserved? What choices have you made to live up to this billing?

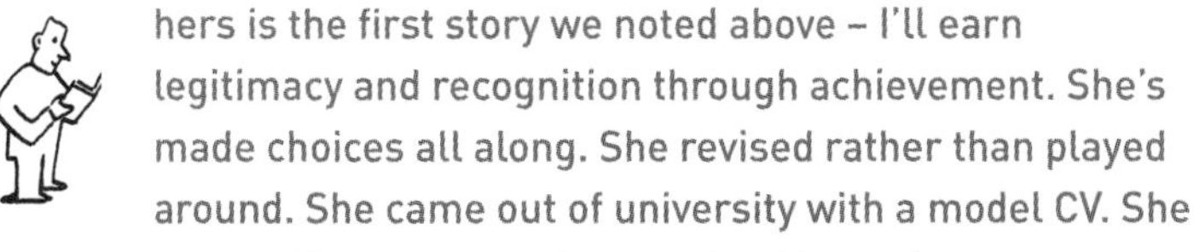

Caroline works in a City legal firm. Professional, smart, funny, hers is the first story we noted above – I'll earn legitimacy and recognition through achievement. She's made choices all along. She revised rather than played around. She came out of university with a model CV. She worked incredible hours and got noticed by senior partners.

She's fortunate to have a secure home life and loving partner, but as she hits 30 she's finding the demands of this theme increasingly difficult. It's just like wanting to be rich, she says.

No-one wants to be rich *per se* – they just want to be richer than they are now. It's the same for her and her appetite for success. When will she feel recognized, she asks? When she does an even bigger deal? Gets an even better paid job?

The interest, even admiration, we have for a character is based on the extent to which they will defend what they believe will endure. You know where you stand with them. This is probably why we hold most politicians in contempt.

A skeleton script

A writer needs a skeleton script – the barest outline of what actually happens to the main character. Let's take things on from the age of 16.

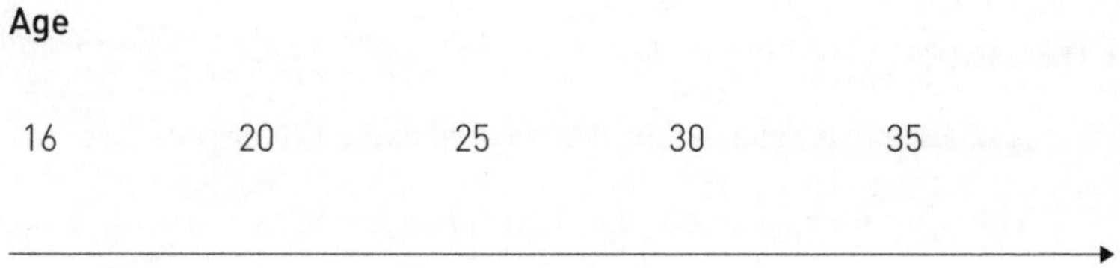

Age

16 20 25 30 35

Imagine the line is your life. At certain key points along it, things happened to you or you made them happen. There are clues here about your character and story. Where did you make choices about what you believed should endure in your life? And where did you end up making no choice at all?

Circumstances might include:

- Whether to continue with a relationship or friendship
- Whether to take or stay in a particular job

- Whether to have children
- Whether to move to a different part of the country, or new country
- Whether to go to college, or which college
- Whether to pursue a particular path of spiritual or personal development

When you've done the lifeline, take a moment to reflect on it. What is the thread?

Conflict

Conflict can happen at many levels: within your mind, between you and other individuals, between you and other parts of the world (the church, the System, the environment).

The interesting thing here is the conflict taking place within you, or between you and others, in pursuit of your active value. As we said before, if there is no conflict, if you are not engaging any forces of antagonism, then there is no story, no dynamic. You, and others, will switch off.

As humans, we're fundamentally lazy. We tend not to risk more than we have to, nor change if we don't have to. We have to engage with forces that oppose what we want to do, in order to be fully realized. We need forces that thwart our will in order for us to know our will. Look at what happened to Lester Burnham in the previous chapter. Only in conflict, with himself, his family and his boss, did he rekindle what felt good about himself.

In the next chapter, we'll look at how this works for Erin Brockovich.

In the meantime, take a look at how this works for you. Conflict is multi-layered. Just note down what occurs when you think about what you've wanted to do, and when that was opposed.

“grab your popcorn and notebook,
here comes the opening scene”

Between people

This tends to be where the watchable conflict is. Most films focus on this since it’s the very stuff of being human. There are innumerable scenes in each of our lives and I’m not going to try and guess what yours might have been. Some of them may be on the skeleton script we created earlier. Here are some that people have told me would form part of their movie.

Remember, each scene features some form of conflict between you and another person or persons. The important thing to explore is why this is strong in your memory. What is it telling you about your story and how does it play a part? How does it relate to the active value we established above?

Some scenes will be positively charged for you and some will be negative, for example:

- The night I argued with my Dad about what kind of job I should have.
- When I screamed at my Mum that I thought she loved my sister more than she loved me.
- When I fought my best friend in the playground for 15 minutes, surrounded by boys chanting ‘Fight’.
- When my college girlfriend left me for someone else.
- When my lover died and I raged at him for leaving me.
- When I resigned from my job because of the way I was treated.
- When I overcame shyness to ask someone out.
- When I was passed over for promotion.

- When my husband found out I was having an affair.
- When I started my company and four banks turned me down before someone backed me.
- When I was made redundant by the same person that had hired me.
- The day we won the rugby match against a better, meaner team.
- When I stood up to a bullying boss.

Inside yourself

The biggest battles are often the forces pitted against each other in your own head. In *The Shawshank Redemption*, Red's most significant conflict is in his own mind. He has become, as a lifer, part of the institution. First, you hate prison, then you grow accustomed to it. Eventually you come to depend upon it. In prison, Red is someone. The outside holds few attractions – and yet he hates himself for thinking this. Prison has sedated him.

As you watch your own film, imagine there's a split screen. In the corner you can read the dialogue going on in your own head as the action unfolds. How does it read in relation to the action? Take a particular scene that feels important. Your first date with someone who became important. A successful job interview.

Probably the most important conflict is between what we feel to be a true action and the saboteur within us.

With others

Somewhere, in everyone's story, there is an encounter with Nemesis. Nemesis is what we fear most, and, in the cause of our active value, *must face*.

“somewhere, in everyone’s story, there is an encounter with Nemesis”

In traditional tales, Nemesis was given the form of a dragon or monster, so that we could have a good clean fight with it, slay it, and get on with life. But these days, it takes different, more intangible forms.

In *The Shawshank Redemption*, because Andy Dufresne’s active value is hope, he meets Nemesis in the form of hopelessness, embodied in the warden. At the film’s lowest point, the Warden, reliant on Andy to launder money for his corrupt schemes, discovers that a fellow prisoner has new evidence that may acquit Dufresne. He has the prisoner shot, and lets Dufresne know that fact just before giving him a month in solitary to brood on it.

In *American Beauty*, Lester’s Nemesis is his neighbour, the man who eventually murders him. Lester’s active value is wonder, of tasting life in all its richness. His neighbour, leading a tight, warped life, storing up volcanic reserves of sexual anger, is his negation.

In the world of business and organizations, we may encounter Nemesis in the form of a boss, colleague or competitor. You know them because you feel fear. They are doing something and you fear its consequences. You end up projecting a lot of emotions on them – most of which, to be frank, are probably unjustified. But there is an inevitability to this.

To live your story, to realize yourself and your active value, you *must* face your own Nemesis. Let’s look at an example.

Mike had worked full on for 13 years, rising to become the country manager of a computer services company. Mike was in the business of sales, and doing whatever he could to encourage individual initiative. He believed in his people and their ability with an infectious fervour. After a year in charge, there were changes at the European level of the company, and a new head of operations, based in the UK, replaced Mike's old boss. Two active values came into conflict – Mike's of entrepreneurship, and his boss's of control. Tighter reins were imposed on negotiating authority, on expenses, on recruitment. Eventually, low-level conflict broke into open warfare in the executive suite.

'Why won't you just back off and let me do my job?!'

'I am letting you do your job – but you need to do it in a different way.'

'You mean your way!'

'If you put it like that, then yes.'

Mike left soon after, and joined a much smaller organization. He missed a lot about corporate life, but rarely missed a sale.

I don't know the rights and wrongs of this situation. Entrepreneurship is no better or worse an active value than control. But the two had to face each other, in order to be realized. Mike is in a better place, for him, and those around him. He can look himself in the mirror in the mornings and he reckons that's more than a lot of his former corporate colleagues. Listen to a senior manager in a telecommunications firm:

'One of the biggest sources of stress here is to maintain an aura of confidence, even when the market's gone to hell and everyone's plans with it. It's bizarre, really, when what we have *to discuss – our own fears about the future, our personal security, our responsibility to our staff – somehow becomes undiscussable. We are facing our worst fear – a meltdown in our business – and we're facing it as a bunch of individuals, not as a team.'*

Pulling it together

Here's a quick aide-mémoire for your work in this chapter.

My theme ....

My active value ....

My character ....

My conflict(s) ....

9

Energy and fear

Where we look at what is vital about us and do our 'dailies'

A reader asks: '**Damn but when is this guy going to start talking about business again?**'

If you don't think that telling a business story is all about energy and fear, then you're not really in business. Keep going. Really.

In the previous chapter we looked at how important conflict is in our lives. We need forces that thwart our will in order for us to know our will. For Lester Burnham, only in conflict – with himself, his family, his boss – did he rekindle what felt good about himself.

It is in engaging with these forces that we realize our own truth: what is vital about us.

Each of us has an energy at our core and in our heart. Yes you do. It is what is *vital* about you. It may be unclear to you, especially if you have spent much of your life avoiding it and its implications. Or it may be that the whole relentless business of life just hasn't given you space to give it voice or opportunity.

Any story, any life worth telling, is based on the conflict between our energy and our fear.

Coping with confllict

One of the modern emblems of female energy is Julia Roberts in *Erin Brockovich*. The phrase 'Life is one damn thing after another' could have been invented for her. Here's where she first encounters George, her eventual lover.

Erin You want my number?

George I do.

Erin Which number do you want, George?

George You got more than one?

Erin Shit, yeah. I got numbers coming out of my ears. Like, for instance, ten.

George Ten?

Erin Sure. That's one of my numbers. It's how many months old my little girl is.

George You got a little girl?

Erin Yeah. Sexy, huh? And here's another: five. That's how old my other daughter is. Seven is my son's age. Two is how many times I been married and divorced. You getting all this? Sixteen is the number of dollars in my bank account. 454-3943 is my phone number. And with all the numbers I gave you, I'm guessing zero is the number of times you're gonna call it.

She turns and heads inside.

Erin has no problem with conflict. In fact, she's turned it into an art form. Life is a fight: a fight for a job, for the money to feed

> *"any story, any life worth telling, is based on the conflict between our energy and our fear"*

and clothe her three children, a fight for dignity, and somewhere in all that, for the love and tenderness we all seek.

One of the strengths of this film as a story is that it captures our struggle to realize ourselves. Like each of us, Erin faces, and faces up to, two levels of conflict. The first is with her external demons – a company and power structure that has poisoned families in a California town. The second is with her internal demons: the pursuit of justice for these families is the pursuit of justice for her own damaged family and sense of self. In righting a wrong externally, she is doing work to heal herself.

There is a parallel in *The Silence of the Lambs*. Clarice Starling, the FBI agent investigating a serial murderer, Buffalo Bill, enters an unholy pact with the imprisoned Hannibal Lecter. He agrees to help her find the murderer but his part of the deal is access to Clarice's past. The brilliance of the structure here is that Starling does the sleuthing on the main plot – finding the murderer. Lecter, on our behalf, does the sleuthing in her unconscious.

Starling is haunted by a childhood episode where, after the murder of her father, she is sent to live on a relative's farm, and is awoken one morning by the screaming of lambs going to the slaughter. She tries to rescue one but fails. She still wakes up in the night, the lambs screaming. It is Lecter's supreme moment of reward to discover this . . . .

Lecter And if you find this girl [*kidnapped by Buffalo Bill*], you think you will stop those lambs screaming, is that right, Clarice?

One of the things that makes a story great is the interplay between the action on screen and the doubt (fear) in the mind. If there were

> *conflicts you face between your energy or truth and the obstacles to its achievement*

no decisions to make or dilemmas to face, the story would lack any tension. And this is also paralleled in our own lives. We constantly encounter the tension between our energy and our fear.

Ever wondered why a film or book works so strongly for you yet leaves someone else untouched? The chances are that it was littered with clues about the conflicts you face between your energy or truth and the obstacles to its achievement.

Sometimes this is clear. *Bridget Jones's Diary* was a tale for any woman who's ever wondered where Mr Right was going to spring from. Sometimes it's not so clear, especially when the story may have a darker or open-ended structure. *Life Is Sweet* by Mike Leigh is the story of a set of people whose lives are half-lived, then further disturbed by the attempt of an adopted young woman to discover the identity of her mother. There is an optimistic ending, but the echo in the audience's heart is of the consequences of denying ourselves the full range of life, and how expertly we chain ourselves to unhappiness.

The obstacles to our vitality or truth loom so large that we may be content not to face them. Yet there is no contentment, for the turning away will cause more pain than the encounter.

I was gonna be someone

Back to Erin.

Erin I don't know what happened to me . . . I mean I was Miss Witchita for Christ sakes. Did you know you were living next door to a real live fucking beauty queen? (*wipes her nose*) I still got the tiara. I thought it meant I was gonna do something important with my life, that I was gonna be someone.

The arc of Erin's story is that of anyone who suffers or who feels that the world may cave in on them. It is for those who carry the load of the choices they've made, or have been made for them.

Summary: what we're learning here

American Beauty teaches us about the role of a protagonist – discovering your vitality and truth and exercising them to the full.

Erin Brockovich shows us how external conflicts are often paralleled by internal ones. We go in pursuit of dragons to quell the ones within us. Stories touch us because they remind us of the mystery of our own drives and demons and offer an experience of how they can be faced.

This book isn't about trying to help you wrestle those inner demons to the floor. It is encouraging you to find those stories that connect with you, and to seek clues and strength from them. Here are some excerpts from email or live conversations I've had with viewers of these films. From differing angles, they are all talking about the story's battle between energy and fear, and how it has a parallel in their own lives.

'She [Erin] has that ability to do what we all wish we could – to screw up her nerves in a little tight ball and make the world listen to her. I know how I shirk from just putting myself on the line in the way she does. One of my favourite parts of the film is where she just starts working at the law firm – you know, she just turns up, no application or interview or anything, then negotiates her terms halfway through the first day.'

'I think we identify with her [Erin] because she's powerful yet fragile. We know she could break at almost any time, and that makes her all the more compelling – that's how we feel, or I feel, if I'm embarking on something that's really testing me – that I could break at any moment.'

'She's my hero – she's the feistmeister!'

“we spend a lot of time living in prisons of our own making”

‘I watched American Beauty *a couple of times, without really understanding why it had haunted me so. Thinking now about it, I believe it’s about the line when Lester says, “In some ways I’m dead already.” We spend a lot of time living in prisons of our own making, and what I love about this movie is how he just walks out, looks back and says, “Why did I ever spend so much time in there?”.’*

‘For men, American Beauty *has so many angles. There’s the freedom in stopping walking on egg shells with women, in not kowtowing to your work, how delicious being irresponsible is. You know, it’s every bit as much of an escape from prison film as* The Shawshank Redemption.*’*

The heart of any strong story is where fear is faced. Screenwriters call this antagonism. In stories, the conflict between energy and fear is staged in a series of tests. The satisfaction of a story is that the conflict is eventually closed – there is an ending. We can close the book, leave the cinema.

Breaking out of the briefcase

Life, however, isn’t Hollywood. Rarely do we face our demon, vanquish him / her and return from the forest happy ever after. Life’s a series of them. Every day we write the book. We never quite resolve the conflict between our energy and our fear, although we can use this tension productively. A briefcase existence is one where you simply oscillate between what you fear and what is vital about you. In a briefcase existence, what is best about you is left expertly boxed in.

The psychologist and writer Dorothy Rowe maintains that there are two basic fears, which derive from the kind of person you tend to be:

“in a briefcase existence, what is best about you is left expertly boxed in”

1. If you’re more introverted (like me) you prefer to try and make sense of the world in your own head, and test that understanding out on the world. Your most basic fear is of chaos, that people and things are random and unpredictable. Agony is not seeing a pattern.
2. If you’re more extroverted, you try to make sense of the world by engaging with other people, and letting that experience help you form your views. Your most basic fear is that people will withdraw from you, not be there with you, making life unbearable. Agony is not being loved.

I think this is a bit broad-brush, since I’m terrified of not being loved as well as everything else, but it is helpful.

It’s important to know what you fear, as well as what is vital for you. If you don’t, it’s difficult to be a protagonist for anything. Uncovering this will required the teensiest bit of reflection. Bear with me. I don’t like this stuff either.

What are you looking at?

A key tool of the film director is the ‘dailies’ – film that has been shot that day. It’s a way of understanding how things are progressing within the bigger story. How did this scene work? Does it advance the story? Does it have emotional truth? Is it building character?

Sit yourself down, Barry Norman like, in front of the big screen. This showing is just for you. It’s your life. Grab your popcorn and notebook. Here comes the opening scene . . .

Since living is a daily business, let’s use this idea. We’ll limit it to a work situation for now. Take a day, any day. Draw two big circles. Title one energy and one fear.

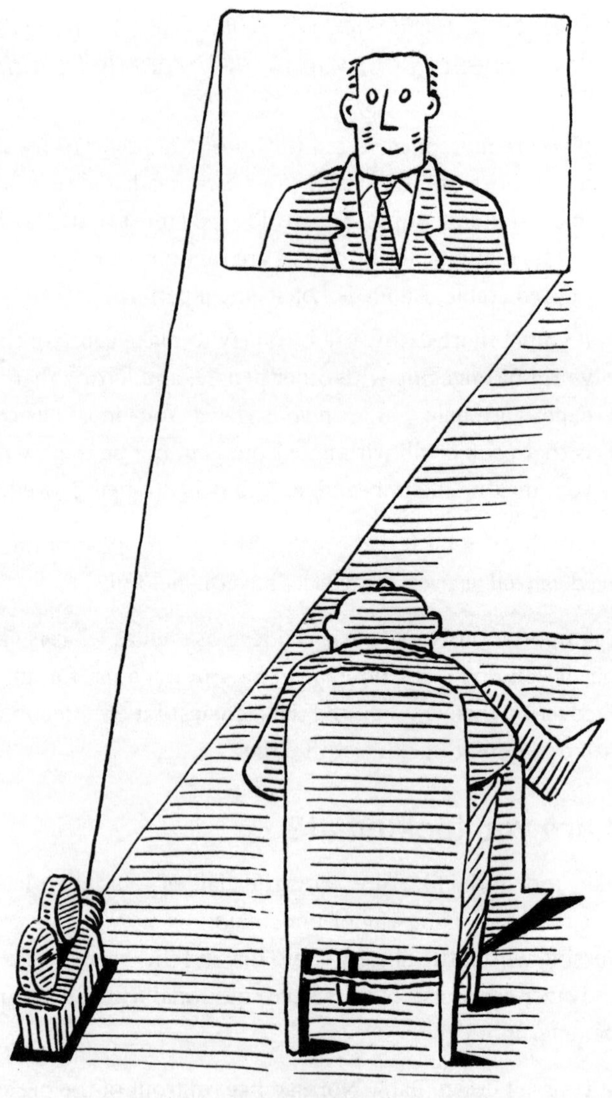

Do your dailies

Step 1 The energy scene

In the first circle, note down, or sketch (stick people are good) a moment in your day when you experienced a sense of energy or truth. I can't tell you how you know when you're feeling this – I'll trust that you know. It could have been in a conversation with someone. It could have been in your own head (for us introverts, it often is). You discovered something that felt important, you did something that felt right for who you are. You were in tune with the universe, if only for a moment. Here are a couple of examples.

'It probably sounds a bit petty, but I'm looking at me crossing the last thing off my list. I love to complete things, to do the stuff I set myself to do. I felt good about it.'

'I'm looking at myself and two colleagues laughing as we brainstorm different ideas about a client's business. It feels easy, productive.'

Now bring this scene to mind – imagine it playing in front of you. Look, listen, sense it.

Now apply two simple questions to this scene. Why does this feel right or feel true to me and my story? Secondly, what would a good and generous friend say it says about me?

Go on, give it a go. It's a cracking exercise. It helps you identify what, at work, you're living for. And that's worth knowing.

Step 2 The fear scene

In this circle, try to identify a moment where you felt fear, or its cousins doubt, uncertainty and concern. What was the situation? Who or what was involved? Where did you feel it in your body? A couple of examples.

'I was on the phone to this customer, and he was really curt, impatient. He wanted a set of results that we'd promised, but couldn't yet give. I'm looking at myself grimacing on the phone, scribbling away, with an irrational sense of failure, of having not kept my word.'

“in fact, fear is essential. It’s there to tell you what’s getting in the way of your own story”

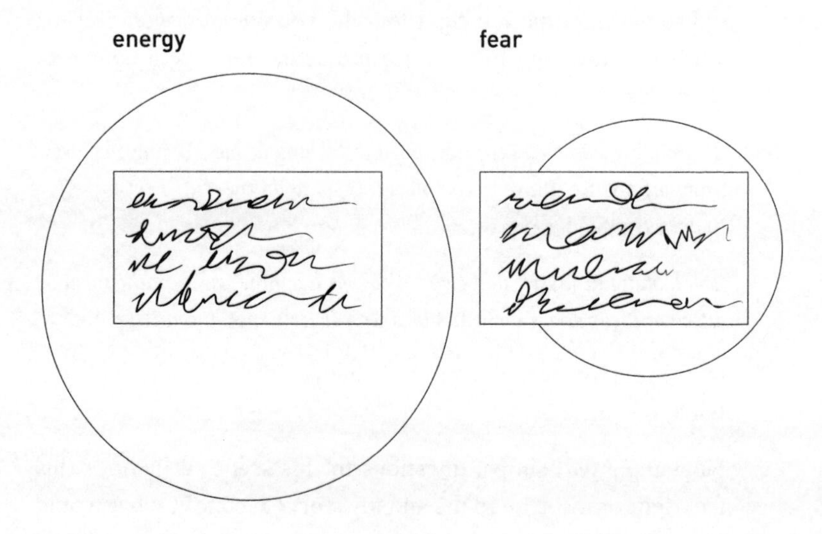

‘I’m looking at myself trying to write this proposal, and just getting distracted all the time, knowing I’ll get to the end of the day and then having to finish it tonight so I can meet the deadline.’

Now bring this scene to mind and imagine it playing in front of you. Look, listen and sense it.

Accept that you felt, and are feeling fear. It’s fine. It’s a recurring feature of all our lives and nothing to be ashamed of. In fact, fear is essential. It’s there to tell you what’s getting in the way of your own story.

Now ask similar questions. Why am I feeling scared or uncertain in this scene? What is at stake? What is it I fear I will lose or have damaged here? What does my good and generous friend tell me?

Step 3 Their relationship

These 'dailies' or snapshots tell you something about the tension between your energy and fear as it exists within your work. Try doing them for three days, consecutively if you can.

You'll get three insights for your story.

The first is how you feel energy and vitality at work. This is precious stuff. It is live evidence of what feels good and true to you.

The second is a clearer sense of what you fear, and what may be blocking your energy and truth.

The third is the relationship between the two. What you love and fear are part of the same pattern, and doing more of what you love (your active value) involves working with what you fear or doubt about yourself (the antagonists).

The two are either in productive tension – you understand and use them – or you are oscillating between them, leaving you powerless.

Here are a couple of people's thoughts after working with this idea.

'As a designer, I love expression and creation, but fear deadlines and constraint (and the people who bring them). I love the opening of possibilities, and hate their closing down because of time pressure. The story here is of trying to make time my friend – of recognizing that my freedom is enhanced because of constraint. With no boundaries I'm lost. Complete freedom of expression is a fantasy. I still want it though!'

'Looking at my dailies, I see a pattern of loving order and completion in my projects, and fretting about contact with the clients of these projects. I'm getting to thinking that without them, I don't get the opportunity to do what I love, and that good contact with them, even if it makes me nervous, is the most important part of what project managing is. It's not easy to make this tension a productive one, but I'll have to.'

> *"every day brings its challenge between our active value or energy, and what opposes it"*

Summary

The essence of story is a conflict between what is vital about us and what we fear. A film or novel dramatizes this, and leaves us with a powerful conclusion.

But for those of us in the trenches of daily life, this conflict is ever present. Every day brings its challenge between our active value or energy, and what opposes it. Mostly, we create what opposes it in our own head.

Being aware of each of these is the first step to creating a productive tension. Prize your energy and live with your fear. It will become ever less relevant.

The playout track of *Erin Brockovich* is *Every Day Is A Winding Road,* by Sheryl Crow. And for good reason.

Every day is a winding road
I get a little bit closer.

It's true. Every day you get a little bit closer. Sometimes, it might be tough to believe this. Sometimes, it will be tough to remember where you're heading. And, often, Stuff will throw you off course. But stay with it. Think Erin, think Lester, think Andy Dufresne.

Think you.

Good luck.

Appendix 1

Very useful stories

Getting more

A fisherman and his brother were relaxing by the quayside, having a beer. They'd sold that day's catch at the market, and were enjoying some down time in the late afternoon sun. A businessman on holiday approached them.

'Listen, you could really clean up round here, guys.'

'How's that?' asked the elder brother.

'The fishing's great round here. I'm thinking we do something together. I'll put up some money for another boat and you could get two out there.'

'What would that do for us?'

'Well, you could earn more, get a better price on gear, get more money at the market. Pretty soon, you could build up the business – hey you could have a fleet!'

'What would that do for us?'

'You'd watch the money come in, do less fishing for a start!'

'What would that do for us?'

'You could sit back, relax, enjoy the sun.'

The elder brother adjusted his hat against the glare, drained the last of his beer and gazed out to sea.

'Enjoy your holiday,' he said to the businessman.

The Horse on the Road

One day, when Erickson was a young man, a horse wandered into his family's yard. The horse had no identifying marks, and no one seemed to know whom it belonged to. Despite this, Erickson offered to try and return the horse to its owners.

He got on the horse and rode it back to the road. He let the horse decide which way it wanted to go. From time to time the horse wandered off the road or stopped to graze in a field. Only on these occasions did Erickson intervene by gently directing the horse back onto the road.

Eventually, the horse stopped outside a farmhouse, several miles down the road. The farmer came out, thanked Erickson for returning him and asked 'How did you know that was our horse and that he belonged here?'

'I didn't,' said Erickson, 'but the horse did. All I had to do was keep him on the road.'

The Captain and the Rabble

During one of the many nineteenth-century riots in Paris, the captain of an army platoon received orders to clear a city square by firing at the *canaille* (rabble).

He commanded his soldiers to take up firing positions, their rifles levelled at the crowd. As a ghastly silence descended, he drew his sword and shouted at the top of his voice, 'Mesdames, messieurs, I have orders to fire at the *canaille*. But as I see a great number of honest, respectable citizens before me, I request that they leave so that I can safely shoot the *canaille*.'

The square was empty within three minutes.

The Shoe Salesmen

In an effort to expand their international sales earlier this century, a shoe company sent two of its young salespeople to developing countries to assess the state of the market. They received two telegrams back:

1 Bad news, stop. None of natives wear shoes.

2 Good news, stop. None of natives wear shoes.

Hitachi

In the doldrums of the recession of the 1970s, Hitachi's Japanese factories making TVs went on short time. Workers repainted the building, fixed the gardens, cleaned the machinery. The senior

managers got more and more anxious. Eventually the supervisors confronted the senior management and stated that their situation was becoming intolerable, and the managers' anxiety wasn't helping. There was no production to manage, because there was no demand.

How could they create demand? There was none coming from Japan, so it would have to come from abroad. A group of the managers formed the first international sales team in that Hitachi division. The rest is history.

The Travelling Monk and Cathedral

The story is told of a monk, who, after spending seven years serving his apprenticeship in the monastery, is told to go and see something of the world.

In his travels, he came upon a scene on the outer edges of a city. Vast numbers of workmen were spread across fields, huge boulders of stone and planks of wood littered the scene. The monk approached a workman, who was busily hammering into one of the bigger boulders.

'What's going on here?' asked the monk.

Not looking up, the workman answered, 'Don't know, mate, all I've been told is that I've got to break this rock up.'

The monk wandered through the site, stopping by another similarly employed man.

'What's happening here?' he asked again.

'Not sure, but I do know that I've got to produce six blocks roughly the same size as those guys' by tomorrow.'

Unenlightened, the monk moved on to the centre of the scene, asking the question of another workman. This man stopped, put his hammer down, and greeted the monk.

'Well, you see that spot 50 feet in front of you? That's where the altar will be, which is what I'm sorting here. We're building a cathedral, you see.'

The Copywriter

Things should be as simple as they can be, said Einstein. A devotee of this was a Joe, a writer I used to work with. Joe's job was to create advertising posters. He understood that for a poster to work as someone drove past it, it had to be clear and arresting. I would try and understand the client's business and product, then brief him, submitting to his endless questions. He'd then disappear off for a couple of days and come back with a brilliant three-word slogan, capturing the essence of the idea with wit and boldness.

'That's fantastic, Joe,' I (and the client) would say. He'd slouch there, shaking his head.

'I'm not happy. It's too long.' And off he would disappear.

A few days later he'd appear. Deadlines for print were nearing. Nerves were getting frayed. Joe wandered in. The slogan was inspiringly condensed into a two-word pistol shot. There was spontaneous applause.

'It's not there, yet,' he said, scratching three days' beard growth.
Two days later, with client in a near frenzy and printers banging on the door, a fax spat out one, perfect word. The cover note was from Joe: 'I'm happy now'.

John Varley's Trousers

(There are many tales of the leaders of organizations. This is possibly because of the authority we give them, in practical and psychological terms. They can often feel remote and , for their own good, need humanizing.)

A few years back, I was doing some work for Barclays. One of the pivotal figures then, and now, was a man called John Varley. Tall, perceptive and incisive, John was distinguished by his beautifully tailored suits and braces. To those who didn't know him, however, his height and power could make him seem somewhat remote.

As part of a change initiative, John spoke at an informal gathering of Barclays' management. This took place at a cinema, and all the speakers were asked to wear polo shirts to indicate that the mood was to be taken lightly.

John stood up to speak and the audience quietened, expecting a sharp disquisition on the state of the industry. His first words were these:
'You know, my most important job here is, in the absence of my braces, to stop my trousers falling down.'

He brought the house down, and his words kicked around the bank for many months, showing how an apparently austere figure was as human as the rest of us.

The Prince and the Magician

(A tale from John Fowles' novel, The Magus. *It has many meanings, but I always take from it the lesson that we are almost always under somebody else's spell.)*

Once upon a time there was a prince who believed in all things but three. He did not believe in princesses, he did not believe in islands, and he did not believe in God. His father, the king, told him such things did not exist. As there were no princesses or islands, in his father's domain, and no sign of God, the young prince believed his father.

One day, the prince ran away from the palace. He came to the next land. There, to his astonishment, from every coast he saw islands and on these islands, strange and troubling creatures that he dared not name. As he was searching for a boat, a man in full evening dress approached him along the shore.

'Are those real islands?' asked the young prince.

'Of course they are real islands,' said the man in evening dress.

'And those strange and troubling creatures?'

'They are all genuine and authentic princesses.'

'Then God must also exist!' cried the prince.

'I am God,' replied the man in full evening dress, with a bow.

The young prince returned home as quickly as he could.

'So you are back,' said the king his father.

'I have seen islands, I have seen princesses, I have seen God,' said the prince reproachfully. The king was unmoved.

'Neither real islands, real princesses nor a real God exist.'

'I saw them!'

'Tell me how God was dressed.'

'God was in full evening dress.'

'Were the sleeves of his coat rolled back?'

The prince remembered that they had been. The king smiled.

'That is the uniform of a magician. You have been deceived.'

At this, the prince returned to the next land and went to the same shore, where once again he came upon the man in full evening dress.

'My father the king has told me who you are,' said the young prince indignantly. 'You deceived me last time, but not again. Now I know that those are not real islands and not real princesses because you are a magician.'

The man on the shore smiled.

'It is you who are deceived, my boy. In your father's kingdom there are many islands and princesses. But you are under your father's spell, so you cannot see them.'

The prince returned pensively home. When he saw his father he looked him in the eyes.

'Father, is it true that you are not a real king, but only a magician?'

The king smiled and rolled back his sleeves.

'Yes, my son, I am only a magician.'

'Then the man on the shore was God.'

'The man on the shore was another magician.'

'I must know the real truth, the truth beyond magic.'

'There is no truth beyond magic,' said the king.

The prince was full of sadness. He said, 'I will kill myself.' The king, by magic, caused Death to appear. Death stood at the door and beckoned to the prince. The prince shuddered. He remembered the beautiful but unreal islands and the unreal but beautiful princesses.

'Very well,' he said, 'I can bear it.'

'You see, my son,' said the king, 'you too now begin to be a magician.'

Walt and the Bankers

(This is true. I can't imagine pitching an idea to more than 20 bankers, let alone 300. 'If at first you don't succeed, quit. No use being a damn fool about it', W.C. Fields.)

When he was trying to find backing for his first theme park, Walt Disney took his plans to over three hundred banks before he got support.

Dale's Temper

This tale is from Steve Biddulph's *The Secret of Happy Children*. Read it a couple of times, because it's more subtle than it seems.

Vera recounts how her 8-year-old, Dale, had developed, ever so gradually, a temper that had become a problem to him and to other people. After one particular blow-up, Vera had given the matter some careful thought and set about an original solution.

She took down an old dusty album of family photos (never seen by the children) and she and Dale looked through them. Vera pointed out the various family patriarchs: Grandfather Les, Great Uncle Alf, cousin Derek – where they had lived and what they had done. Vera provided the narrative. 'Alf was a good bloke, but very stubborn. Grandfather had a real temper as a boy, so they say.' There was a pause as Dale wondered where this was leading. Vera just turned the pages. 'What happened to his temper, Mum?' 'Oh he just grew out of it, I guess. Look here's his cricket team . . .'

Soon the other children came in and Vera left them with the photos and went to get tea. Dale, though, of course, he could be pretty stubborn, never really lost his temper again. Just grew out of it, I guess.

Appendix 2

Unsticking other bits of life

In this section, I thought it would be good to cast our eyes away from the immediate area of work, and look at other parts of life. After all, you may want to influence someone other than your immediate work colleagues or a customer. At least, I hope so.

You may seek to influence your children, your partner, your community, your friends. Because if you aren't tempted to influence them in some way, you have to question what your role is.

So let's go from the assumption that you're trying to influence things for good. Let's assume you're trying to teach your children some basic values that will help them navigate their way in the world. Let's assume you're trying to nurture a sense of community in your neighbourhood or town. Let's assume you're building a stake in the future, and need to influence people to make that real.

By using story, you are constructing a world that they can imagine, so that they will walk willing in.

I'd like to look at two areas: children and community.

Children

Earlier in the book, we touched on how stories had a unique power in providing examples of constancy: of how certain things endure. This is precisely what youngsters enjoy. In listening to a story, they develop that sense of inner time and place; the place, as adults, we invite others into as part of influencing them.

I'm no idealist about children. I'm writing this at 8.30 on a Saturday morning while my wife rounds up two squealing squawking girls as they attempt to colonize as much space and attention as humanly possible.

But children need, indeed, they crave our influence. At every stage of their lives up to and including adolescence, they need stories and examples that give them clues as to how they should be living, and how they can gain purchase on what feels like a precarious existence. Stories are one of the fundamental ways we reassure them about life.

This isn't straightforward. Right from the word go, we start reading them all sorts of barbarous nonsense. Have you ever listened to nursery rhymes? 'Ring A Ring A Roses': a little Black Death ditty. 'Humpty Dumpty': failed attempt by the military to resolve suicidal egg-type person situation. 'Rock A Bye Baby': abandoned child dies in tragic fall.

Then we get onto fairy tales, and a succession of blood-thirsty pirates, dark forests, wolves, goblins and monsters. Anyone who's read these scrunched up with a toddler is familiar with the clenching and screaming that accompanies a good read.

What's going on? I think the answer is that we are using the story as a safe container for exploring the dangers and joys of life. Crucially, we're doing it next to them, cuddled up at bedtime. The story may have a reassuring end, but more importantly, the reassurance is provided by the person you're still next to, who closes the book, gives you a hug and kisses you goodnight.

There are any number of types of stories we tell our children, but here are some examples garnered from limited experience. I'd put them in random order until Liz, my wife, dropped a great book by Steve Biddulph, called *The Secret of Happy Children* into my lap. (Honestly, it is terrific. I wish I'd read it when I was 4. Would have saved a lot of heartache.)

Age	**Effective storytelling**
0–6 months: Can I trust these people?	What you're doing here, so naturally that you don't even realize it, is establishing basic ideas like time (past, present and future) and cause/effect through narrative. We make mini dramas out of daily events – nappies, feeding, movement, greetings. In doing so, we develop in our children that inner world of sensation and mystery which will always be available to them via story or other art.
6–18 months: Explore!	This is where children start to educate themselves, normally at the expense of your home and its contents. The most effective stories are those that encourage them to channel their developing language and motor skills: song, movement, textured books with pop-up or audio features. There's a wonderfully ritualized element to the basic nursery rhymes, and to books such as Mary Murphy's *I Like It When*, or Virginia Miller's series featuring a toddler bear called Bartholemew. Also I'd encourage you to be the storyteller you naturally are with your child. It only takes a small imaginary leap to take your toddler's favourite bear or bath toy into an

	adventure. Not much of an adventure either. For most toddlers, their toy walking around them then jumping down their t-shirt beats a £15 video or the Telly Tubbies hands down.
18 months to 3 years: Learning to think	Welcome to the 'terrible twos'. This phrase is such a byword for misbehaviour that a parent will smile wanly at you after her toddler has taken a hunk out of your/your child's/your dog's thigh and say, 'I'm sorry, he's two' and expect you to grin obligingly. There are no end of books that will stimulate the imagination and provide parallels to the child's central question, about where the boundaries are in life. They are all variants on the central idea of teaching us how to behave by using example. This is a useful strategy, because unless you're really smart, you don't stand much of a chance of explaining to a 2/3-year-old why she shouldn't do something (say, push over a small friend) if there isn't any obvious physical consequence. She hasn't got the mental equipment. You can begin to get it across by example or parallel, describing how Winnie the Pooh treats his friends, or even how one of her nursery pals treats hers. Mothers, often of larger families, are capable of weaving brilliant parables about a child's friends, family or even pets to teach simple rules of behaviour.
3–6 years: Other people	This is where children have to come to terms with the fact that they live with, rather than just alongside other people. Much storytelling at this stage is an extension of the above strategy – edging

them into the civilized world by smuggling in a few basic standards. And I use the word 'smuggle' deliberately. Remember earlier how we discovered the basic rule of stimulus–response? That if you wanted to influence someone, the last thing you should tell them is the response you want? Well, it's at about this stage that kids' antennae start to get used to clumsy communication. They can spot a fake.

Some children's authors are particularly gifted at this smuggling in of the lesson. Helen Cooper's books transport children and adults into new worlds, and my kids love H.A. Rey's *Curious George* series.

Even though they're more practised, I think children at this age also respond even more strongly to participating in a story being 'made' in the moment. You can give them characters, whether animals, themselves, princes, elves and fairies, and then either lead the narrative or get them to take it on. The fun and tension in the moment is a precursor of the times in adult life when we realize we have to take responsibility for our own story. More importantly, it's great fun.

6–12 years:
I did it my way

In the words of Steve Biddulph, 'what makes it possible for a 6- to 12-year-old to navigate the world of school, friends and life generally is his or her knowledge of the way things work and the "rules of life" . . . Parents will help by being firm on those rules that are important, but negotiating and compromising on those that are negotiable.'

There's a story from Biddulph's book in Appendix 1 which is a brilliant example of

	artful parenting. I think its lesson is that much of this phase is about finding powerful and subtle ways to enforce the rules that the child will probably be clear on by this stage. As that rather irritating book said, all you really need to know you learn in kindergarten anyhow.
12–18 years: Getting ready to leave	I shouldn't bother. Beyond the pale, most of them. Drive them where they want to go, and keep shtum while you're at it.

Community action

I'm using this as a catch-all term for things outside your front door but away from work. (Just in case you've had a sudden attack of guilt realizing that you don't even know your neighbour's name.) I'm also implying that your action in the community is to influence things in a particular direction.

Examples of community action

- Being part of a PTA or support network for a school
- Raising funds for a local hostel – or even a far away one
- Campaigning for global debt relief
- Re-instating flogging of criminals in public places (hey, whatever toasts your teacake)
- Working for a church or belief
- Getting a playground built or a local park improved
- Stopping unwanted development, from local roadworks to a new Terminal 5

All these activities have one thing in common. You are dealing with existing power and belief structures, which you want to influence. When you're dealing with local issues, and especially local politicians, it's easy to forget the golden rule of influence: don't confuse the stimulus with the response.

Most arguments about power and politics are sterile exchanges. Try watching BBC Parliament for more than three minutes if you don't believe me.

Much of this comes about because we are stuck in what Edward de Bono calls 'rock logic'. It is the logic of our traditional thinking patterns, where we pop things into categories that seem clear and hard-edged – like a rock. 'Water logic' is a different strategy, and type of thinking. Water is just as real as rock, but different. It flows. The emphasis of water logic is where things are going, not just what is. What happens next, in fact.

Let's use a story to illustrate this, comparing the reaction of two shop assistants in a US store. A shopper came back to return a chicken ready meal. Assistant A's response was rock-like – and logical. 'We can't do an exchange, because we don't even sell that brand, ma'am.' The assistant was concerned with the rules and what 'is'. The shopper moved on, and took the same request to another assistant. 'Certainly, madam. Try this one, it's similar, although slightly tastier.' The second assistant was using water logic, which is concerned with what a situation leads to, not just what is. She was applying the idea that a piece of good customer service would lead to loyalty, as all the research suggests it does. In the US store, this ethic is known as Give The Woman A Chicken, which I think gets over the idea nicely.

So when things are heated, as they can be in power and politics, an influencer's route will often be that of water logic – using emotion, story and humour to help describe what the situation could lead to, rather than rehearsing what is.

One of the most powerful pieces of communication I ever heard was a resident at a local council meeting. The issue at stake was the building of a new road through an existing residential settlement. There were lots of strong points to be made on both sides. But the meeting was swayed by an older man. He simply said this. 'The piece of land we are talking about was, in my youth, converted from wasteland into an orchard. The orchard went, because the land was needed to build homes for people. And then the space became a little more crowded, because more homes were needed. And these are good things. I live there, and I have a home, because we made these decisions. But I now ask where will this lead? We needed an orchard, we needed homes. But do we really need another road? Will we look at this decision in 20 years' time, and say, "Did we need to do this?" I just wonder.'

Whether he crafted it deliberately or naturally (you'll notice the natural cadence of beginning, middle and end) I don't know. I do know that the vote went his way, without his getting into the 'I Am Right You Are Wrong' game that so often plagues our communities.

So, whatever your cause, whether you are canvassing neighbours, councillors or the might of the corporate world, remember that they are susceptible. Use your skill to paint a picture of what their actions will lead to, rather than engaging them on their own ground. It's a kind of judo: rather than just oppose someone's weight, play a different game. Lever their interests and beliefs to your own advantage, and enjoy the results.

OTHER BOOKS TO MAKE YOU BETTER...

Personal Skills

The Rules of Work

A definitive code for personal success

Richard Templar 0 273 66271 6

This is the definitive code for personal success, while remaining a decent person. For the first time, this book reveals the hidden competitive advantage of 10 immutable laws followed by high achievers worldwide. Give yourself the edge at work – learn to play by The Rules.

Get it, and get on.

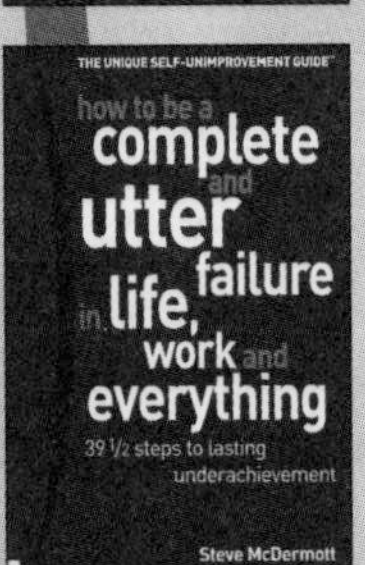

How to be a Complete and Utter Failure in Life, Work and Everything

39½ steps to lasting underachievement

Steve McDermott 0 273 66166 3

This is the ultimate "un-improvement" guide, offering 39½ steps to being a failure using the power of reverse psychology to show you how to be an unqualified success.

How to Manage Your Boss

Developing the perfect working relationship

Ros Jay 0 273 65931 6

Bosses are human – some good, some bad. They have a huge impact on your job satisfaction, your day-to-day happiness, your workload – and yes – your income. If you're lucky they will be understanding, supportive, encouraging and inspiring. Then again they might be lazy, unmotivated, weak, over-emotional, sarcastic, rude, or just downright – well – bossy.

We've all got one. Even the best ones aren't always easy people – and worst case, well, they can make life hell. It's time to learn how to manage them back.

If you wish to find out more about any of these titles visit us at:

www.business-minds.com